STAGE FRIGHT

STEPHEN AARON

Stage Fright

ITS ROLE IN ACTING

The University of Chicago Press
Chicago and London

STEPHEN AARON is a clinical psychologist and an adjunct supervisor of psychotherapy at the City University of New York. He maintains a private practice of adult and adolescent psychotherapy in New York. He has directed more than eighty productions, from classical tragedy to Pinter, and was founder and artistic director of the New Theatre Workshop. Dr. Aaron continues to teach acting at the Juilliard School.

The University of Chicago Press, Chicago 60637
The University of Chicago Press, Ltd., London

© 1986 by The University of Chicago
All rights reserved. Published 1986
Printed in the United States of America

95 94 93 92 91 90 89 88 87 86   5432

Library of Congress Cataloging-in-Publication Data
Aaron, Stephen.
  Stage fright.

  Bibliography: p.
  Includes index.
  1. Stage fright.   2. Acting.   3. Psychoanalysis.
I. Title.
PN2071.P78A27   1986   792'.028   85-24649
ISBN 0-226-00018-4

65938

For my Mother and Father

CONTENTS

PREFACE

My interest in stage fright actually began many years ago: first as an informal attempt to understand it in myself as an actor, later to deal with it as a director, still later as an acting teacher, and finally, in a more systematic way, as a clinical psychologist and psychotherapist. On the basis of such evidence—introspection, natural observation, participant observation, structured and nonstructured interviews—I began to see that the roots of stage fright were to be found in the very nature of the acting process: hence, the title and the structure of this book. Stage fright, at least as far as the performing actor is concerned, is not merely an occupational hazard, an unpleasant side effect of performance: it exists *in* the art of acting. Furthermore, the kind of stage fright I am talking about is more than just a feeling of being keyed up. It is not simply "heightened tension" (Thomas 1982, p. A26). I will be describing very severe anxiety attacks as they have been lived through and conquered by the actor.

An initial decision was made to limit this study to the performing stage actor, partly, of course, because of my own familiarity with the world of the theater. But even a cursory examination of the problems inherent in a study of stage fright in all its manifestations—in the public speaker, the teacher, the politician, the athlete, the musician, the opera singer, the dancer, and so forth—reveals at once a vast number of variables that could not be encompassed within the scope of one book. For example, a person stands in front of an audience to present something. The composition of the audience, its expectations, the setting in which the interaction takes place—all such factors would affect the presenter's experience to a significant degree. Moreover, is the "something" presented the speaker's own words and thoughts as one might expect in a classroom lecture? Or is it partly the speaker's thoughts and partly his adviser's thoughts? Or are these the words of a playwright which the speaker must somehow "make his own" and incorporate into the totality of a verbal and physical performance? Has the person made an attempt to memorize his words? Or are there no words at all? Is the event taking place in front of a live audience or in front of a camera? Finally, what are the presenter's expectations and motivations? Is he attempting to entertain, to educate, to persuade, to cajole? Or is it a combination of all these things, as recent political campaigns suggest?

In the face of such a bewildering array of questions, limiting the field of inquiry to one type of public presentation, namely, a play, seemed to offer the best springboard for a study of this complex phenomenon. I hope that the issues addressed in this book will stimulate others to consider different kinds of performance acts.

For example, musicians, singers, and dancers suffer severe anxiety attacks before a performance. The symptoms of such attacks are often similar to those the actor experiences but, as I hope to show, the underlying causes of these attacks, the intrapsychic conflicts that generate the symptoms, are different. I make this assertion based upon my belief that it is only the actor who attempts such a radical transformation of the self into another character. This is not to say that opera singers do not engage in some form of "acting" but that it is of a very different order of intensity. The singer, after all, has to fulfill the vocal demands of the role and so concentration is split between aspects of characterization and vocal technique. The musical score itself imposes stringent limitations on timing, movement, phrasing, and articulation so that the singer does not have the freedom to engage in the kind of "play" I describe in this book. Finally, the presence of the conductor, not to mention the actual sound of the music coming from the orchestra pit, supplies a companionship during performance which the actor does not have. Considerations of this kind seem to separate the actor from other performing artists.

Indeed, another outcome of this study was an understanding of how the actor-director relationship contributes to the stage fright attack itself. But is this unique to the theater? What is the nature of the bond that links the conductor and singer, choreographer and dancer, coach and ballplayer? And what role, if any, does this bond play in the stage fright of these other performers?

Having settled on the stage actor, I had to introduce several other criteria. Actors perform publicly in many different ways: improvisational theater, for instance, makes significantly different demands on the actor than a more conventional presentation does. As a result, I have further limited this study of stage fright to its occurrence during the performance of an already composed text that has been rehearsed for a commercial presentation.

Two terminological notes: first, a play does not exist on paper. "Play" refers to what happens in a theater when actors perform in front of an audience. Strictly speaking, one cannot read a play; one reads a script or a text. A composed text can be thought of as a series of instructions from the playwright to a group of craftsmen: actor, director, set designer, costumer, and so forth. It is a blueprint for action, and in the first two chapters of this book I go to some lengths to describe how an actor makes use of these instructions, decoding them, as it were, into actable terms. Second, "actor" is used throughout to denote both the actor and the actress. This use of "actor" to refer to both sexes seems to be rather common in the theater and inoffensive. I had considered using "performer," but this word is not precise enough and, in fact, blurs a distinction between what we might call "the entertainment value" of a performance and its "acting value."

It also seemed wise to eliminate from this study the reports of student actors and inexperienced professionals. After all, one would expect beginners to experience some form of stage fright because of the newness of performing in public and the career pressures involved in making a start in the acting profession. In fact, this became an important variable to control for, namely, very real concerns that the actor might have about where his next meal was coming from.

Therefore, the actors and directors described in this book are all working professionals: they have had at least ten years' experience in the theater and have not been involuntarily out of work for more than an eight-week period. It turned out, in fact, that the majority were people whom we would all consider truly gifted. In other words, they are not only well known but also well recognized for their talent, whether it be by the theater industry itself or by the community at large as represented, for example, by the New York Drama Critics' Awards or by a knighthood. As a matter of fact, one of the curiosities of stage fright, to say the least, is that it recurs after years of experience or after hundreds of performances of the same part. Obviously, this "curiosity" is one of my major concerns.

Consequently, all those interviewed have been promised complete confidentiality. They are identified by capital letters which remain constant throughout: Actor B stands for the same person whenever he or she is cited. I have changed the names of plays and condensed the sequence of events in order to offer further protection to the actors and directors. This has been necessary because of their "high visibility" in the professional theater.

The word "interview" may be misleading; these talks were not just question-and-answer sessions. But in-depth, nonstructured interviews cannot offer the same degree of certainty about unconscious mental processes that we can get from listening to a patient during the course of an analysis. In this sense, I present no "hard clinical data" in this book. The conclusions I have drawn are based upon a convergence of data. For example, during rehearsals, I watched actors as they tried to cope with stage fright and I also saw that they seemed to establish a particular relationship with me as their director, a relationship that did not appear to be solely in the service of the task at hand. I became, in short, a participant observer, privy to the behavior of actors in the heat of the moment, and began to suspect that there might be some connection between the actor's bond with the director and the onset of the anxiety attack itself. I then started to talk to actors specifically about stage fright and found some of my hunches confirmed. Since I was still directing, I also had the opportunity to use the material from the interviews as guideposts to further investigation during the personal experience of rehearsals and performances. In addition, I watched other directors at work, in some cases following a production from beginning to end. This, then, is what I like to think of as "the hidden methodology" of this book.

In chapters 1 and 2, I describe how an actor prepares and rehearses a play. I have not sought to present my own ideas about how to direct a play or how to act, although I recognize that in an enterprise of this kind my own orientation cannot help but show through in certain places. But the fact is that I do not necessarily endorse a great deal of what I describe, particularly when it comes to matters of directorial technique. This is also not a comprehensive description of rehearsals. First of all, I have emphasized mainly those intrapsychic elements that figure in the actor's attempt to transform himself into the character and that relate to the stage fright attack itself. Because the accent here is on the actor's imaginative life, you may get the unwarranted impression that all actors work, so to speak, from the inside out. This is not so. Some actors will start with the externals of a part—how the character looks, walks, gestures, and talks—but inevitably the gifted actor will connect such exploration with the inner life of the character in order to flesh out the external components of the part.

Second, nothing ever goes quite as smoothly as I describe it, nor do things necessarily proceed in the order I indicate. I have in mind the production of a play in which there are minimal complications: the producer does not interfere with the work, the actor's agent does not give his client suggestions on how to play the part, and the production does not undergo extensive rewriting in the course of out-of-town tryouts. Perhaps the most significant omission in the description of the rehearsal process is the author. He makes a brief entry in chapter 3 but there only to illustrate the supraordinate role of the stage director in the contemporary theater. Although an author's contribution to the success of his play does not end when he turns in the completed manuscript, his comments during rehearsal are usually and properly made to the director and not to any of the actors. Again, this is the ideal: for as many playwrights as one can cite who rigorously adhere to the notion that the director and cast have their own expertise and are best left alone, there are scores of writers who cannot "let go" and attempt to rehearse the play behind the director's back, confusing the actors even more.

I am not unduly troubled by such omissions because, as we will soon see, there is enough stress on the actor even in a smoothly rehearsed play. The introduction of any further complicating factors would only intensify the stress on the actor and, in fact, lend added weight to the argument that the origins of stage fright are ultimately to be found in the acting and rehearsing process.

Furthermore, I have made almost no attempt to take individual differences among actors into consideration. I have, in fact, ignored such differences to emphasize the similarities among actors in their methods of preparation and performance as well as in their ways of coping with stage fright. This has been done to etch out, in stark relief, the psychological processes of stage fright that seem to be common to all experienced actors who work in the contemporary, commercial theater. While this approach has its merits, particularly in a study of this kind, it also carries with it an undeniable area of imprecision. For example, Roy Schafer suggested that a consideration of the regression inherent in stage fright would have to take into account the personality structure of the individual. He alerted us to a crucial distinction between what psychoanalysts call a developmental deficit, that is to say, a part of the mind that never completely matured, and a regression from an already fully structuralized psychic apparatus. In other words, it makes little sense to speak of regression, a movement back toward earlier modes of functioning and thinking, unless we can assume that the person has already progressed to some specifiable level of development (1978, personal communication).

There are, however, two apparently different types of

actor, namely, the British (classical) actor and his American (naturalistic) counterpart. For at least the past forty years a sharp distinction has been drawn between these two acting styles: the British were associated with classical theater, stylized performances, and a somewhat old-fashioned emphasis on technique (voice and body); American acting, on the other hand, was seen as the exclusive domain of naturalistic, inner-directed, psychologically oriented acting. Recent productions from Britain, however, have begun to blur these distinctions. I am thinking of John Gielgud and the late Ralph Richardson in *Home* and *No Man's Land* and, of course, Laurence Olivier in *Long Day's Journey into Night* and *The Entertainer*.

The point is that truly fine acting has always represented a unity of the polarities defined in the contrast of these two styles. Furthermore, my observations of British and American actors have taught me that their inner experience of acting is not significantly different even though the end results may appear to be and, indeed, often are. For instance, a distinguished British actor was directing a production of a classical play. He had been concerned about what he saw as the influence of the American "method" creeping into his younger colleagues' work. When he addressed the cast at the first rehearsal, he said, "You must always remember that acting is simulation, magic, pretense. You must never experience emotion on stage, for then you cease to be an artist. Of course, don't take me as an example. Whenever I'm on stage I cry but that's because I'm so beautiful." This actor, who appears several times in this book, was making a rather complex, albeit flippant and embarrassed, statement about his own understanding of the acting process. In fact, he works in an intensely personal way on each part he plays, using some of Stanislavski's suggestions as guiding principles for his own preparation.

In short, getting beneath the surface has been one of the main goals of this study and it is particularly pertinent for an understanding of stage fright. Any attempt to look at the actor's work from the outside, to look at its results, can only be misleading. There are certain fundamental creative problems that every actor faces—and stage fright is one of them—which transcend surface distinctions.

Chapters 1 and 2, then, set the stage for the main event. Chapter 3 is largely descriptive of what stage fright feels like and how actors try to cope with it. In chapter 4, I attempt to shape a definition of the anxiety attack from a psychoanalytic point of view. Chapter 5 offers an explanation of what triggers stage fright and what its sources are. Because I have written this book with a rather broad audience in mind, that is to say, actors and directors, psychologists and psychoanalysts, not to mention the general theatergoing public, individual readers may find certain sections familiar and even elementary. I ask for their patience; the sense of the familiar will, I hope, provide the specialized reader with a comfortable map before moving into foreign territory.

The choice of a psychoanalytic perspective was not an a priori one. The psychoanalytically informed point of view gradually emerged from an examination of and direct personal experience with the data. As I listened to the actors talk about acting and stage fright, I realized that we were in the realm of dreams and fantasies. Psychoanalysis is the investigative tool par excellence for gaining an understanding of unconscious mental processes and the intrapsychic dynamics of anxiety and certainly for examining the shifts that take place within the actor's mind as he engages in such a radical transformation of self.

In the course of this book, I have tried to render the language of psychoanalysis in terms that will be accessible and immediately meaningful to the general reader. In order to insure the flow of the narrative, I have relegated to the note section certain specific issues that may be of interest only to the psychoanalytically informed reader. (Some of the notes also discuss aspects of rehearsal and performance technique, which will probably be of interest only to actors and directors.) Furthermore, I will make reference to certain intrapsychic mechanisms such as splitting, projection, denial, fusion of the images of the self and others, mechanisms that are seen to be operative in the acting and performing process. But in no way am I assuming that the actor is a representative of a borderline personality organization or of pathological narcissism, implying a lack of cohesion of the self (Kernberg 1975). These concepts are introduced because of their explanatory force, the full impact of which will be felt in chapter 5, where the causes of the stage fright attack are examined in detail.

Finally, by using the concept of "transference" to characterize one aspect of the actor-director relationship, I do not mean to imply that there is anything necessarily therapeutic about this relationship, the rehearsal process, or the performance of a stage play. "Transference" can describe a relationship outside of the (psychoanalytic) therapeutic session. What makes transference unique to psychoanalysis is not that it exists or emerges in treatment but that the analyst interprets it and ultimately resolves it in order to help the patient understand how his present mode of relating to people is based upon earlier experiences with significant others.

Interestingly enough, there are only a handful of articles on stage fright in the psychoanalytic literature; fortunately, they are, in the main, first rate. Most important is the work of Donald Kaplan (1968, 1969) and Glen O. Gabbard (1979, 1983). Although my focus has been on those determinants of stage fright that are part of the acting process itself, what is significant and gratifying is that Kaplan, Gabbard, and I, looking at this phenomenon from different vantage points, have come to similar conclusions. I hope that my debt to them is repaid in some measure by the ways in which I have made careful use of their excellent contributions.

Because we are psychoanalytically oriented observers, we have been trained to look beneath the surface of behavior in an attempt to understand its psychic determinants; we are not content to leave the workings of the mind in "a black box." I think that investigations such as ours can illuminate issues that do not pertain solely to the theater. When "actors talk about acting" (Funke and Booth 1961), we are provided with invaluable data about several major topics that occupy psychoanalytic thought today, particularly the problem of narcissism, the attempt to define the concept of self-representation more precisely, the ways in which transference phenomena manifest themselves outside of the analytic consultation room, and the creative process itself.

Finally, my hope for the actors—the people who have to

live through stage fright and somehow overcome it—is that this study will give them greater courage and greater understanding. This is not a "how to do it" book. Nor is its message ultimately "Grin and bear it." Had this been the case, I might have been tempted to paraphrase the title of one of Stanley Kubrick's films and call this enterprise "Dr. Feelgood, or How I learned to stop worrying and love stage fright." To the contrary, this book attempts to describe and define stage fright in order to show that it is one of the many artistic problems with which the actor must cope as he tries to transform his private dreams into a public reality.

I am indebted to Harper and Row, Publishers, for permission to quote from *The Letters of Sigmund Freud* (Basic Books, 1960).

I want to thank those actors who so generously gave their time to be interviewed. I owe a debt of gratitude to the actors I have directed and taught over the past twenty-five years and to my colleagues at the Theater Center of the Juilliard School in New York, for their informal (and sometimes unwitting) contribution to my understanding of the process of acting. And I owe a significant further debt to my patients, from whom I learn daily about the ordeal of being human.

I benefited greatly from the suggestions of Drs. Arnold Cooper and A. J. Siegman, who read a preliminary communication prepared at a time when I was still interviewing actors. Many of their questions helped focus the later stages of the inquiry on extremely profitable areas. Dr. Roy Schafer gave me the chance to read a paper on stage fright to his ongoing research seminar at New York Hospital's Payne Whitney Clinic, Cornell University Medical Center. The free-for-all that followed was both stimulating and encouraging.

The following people read the manuscript in different stages of its development and offered insightful comments to which I hope I have done justice: Cynthia Friedman, Dr. Jay Harris, Richard Poirier, Marian Seldes, Harold Stone, Dr. Paul Wachtel, and the late Dr. Gilbert Voyat.

I owe Dr. Alan Roland a great deal. He read the manuscript in its first and final drafts, alerting me to the significance of the mother's mirroring function toward her infant. He also offered me the opportunity to present a paper on this topic at a scientific meeting of the National Psychological Association for Psychoanalysis; the discussion afterwards was provocative, particularly in view of Dr. Donald Kaplan's presence on the panel.

Throughout my graduate training, Professor I. H. Paul was successively my adviser, supervisor, and mentor; he also, I am proud to say, has become my friend. His enthusiasm and humor were infectious; his cautionary mini-sermons educated my narcissism. Obviously, Dr. Paul has given this book several close readings, both for content and form.

And, finally, to Linda Tuck, for her generosity, her tough-mindedness, and her refusal to let me stray from the mark for too long, I owe the deepest appreciation of all.

It is good to hear that you are again going to write something about yourself. If I understand correctly, you intend this time to elucidate the secret of your achievement and success, and you imagine that your technique consists in relegating your own person completely to the background and replacing it by the character whom you are representing. And now you wish me to tell you whether this process is likely and whether it applies to you.

I wish I knew more about this process; then I would certainly tell you everything I know. Since I don't understand much about it, I must ask you to be content with the following suggestions. I believe that what you consider the psychological mechanism of your art has been claimed very often, perhaps universally. But this idea of the obliteration of one's own person and its replacement by an imagined one has never quite satisfied me. It tells us so little, doesn't inform us how it is brought about, and above all it fails to explain why one person should succeed so much better than another in achieving what every artist allegedly wants. I rather suspect that an element of the opposite mechanism is indispensable for it: that one's own person is not obliterated but that parts of it—repressed desires and traits that haven't had a chance to develop—are employed to represent the chosen character and in this way find expression and give it the stamp of truth.

—Freud to Yvette Guilbert
8 March 1931

1

THE ACTOR'S WORK
ON HIMSELF

Spencer Tracy does it, that's all. Feels it. Says it. Talks. Listens. He
means what he says when he says it, and if you think that's easy,
try it.

—Humphrey Bogart

The Actor as Instrument

The actor is his own instrument. His physical gestures and
his vocal intonations, not to mention the inner, imaginative
research he has done on the character he portrays, comprise
the product of the actor's creativity. He is both the piano
and the piano player.

Unlike the painter, the poet, and the composer, the actor
cannot readily objectify his own work. The painter can step
back from his canvas and look at what he has done; the poet
and composer can listen to their work. This observing-
evaluating mode of mental functioning is vital to the creative process. As Ernst Kris (1952) outlines it, following a
state of inspiration in which the actual work of creation
takes place, there has to be a state of elaboration when the
artist evaluates what he has created. But the actor lacks the
basic tools for such self-evaluation because he cannot easily
step away from himself. In fact, what he has created
vanishes the moment he stops working.

Consider the intangible aspect of the actor's work as
being akin to this somewhat nightmarish fantasy: a painter

is working on a canvas; the moment he puts down his brush, the painting disappears. The nightmare might continue as follows: in a desperate attempt to keep his creation in front of himself, the painter works with a Polaroid camera to record the product of each day's work so that he would be able to start again the next morning. But even so, he would have to reproduce the previous day's work before he could make additions to other parts of the canvas or revise already completed sections, making the dream absurd as well as anxiety-provoking.

This fantasy dramatizes—in the concreteness of nightmare—the plight of the actor. It focuses attention on a crucial aspect of his dilemma, namely, the necessity of an outside eye to help him remember his work and improve it. For instance, after several run-throughs of a short scene during the second week of rehearsal, a director told the actors that he liked what they had done. It was right for the play as a whole and it made sense as far as their individual characters were concerned. He ended with something like, "That was terrific! Let's keep it in." But with a mixture of pleasure and embarrassment, Actress A responded, "Fine. Now tell me what I've done that's so good. I can't remember." This was followed by nervous laughter from all.

Such interchanges are the rule rather than the exception. Actors have a difficult time remembering what they did in rehearsal. Shortly, I shall be analyzing what *it* is that the actor can't remember; the entire question of memory relates to how the actor prepares, what *it* is he works on. This analysis of the acting process is necessary in order to understand exactly why Actress A couldn't remember and, more interestingly, what she does (or, I might say, chooses to) remember. Suffice it to say that Actress A could remember her lines as well as the moves and gestures she made, but was unable to differentiate, in a more precise or articulated way, among the four or five run-throughs of the scene. Thus, the director had to function for Actress A as the Polaroid camera in the painter's nightmare. At this stage of rehearsal, she had no inner objective representation of her work.

The need for an outside eye becomes compelling when the actor has to evaluate his work. Kris's formulation implies a two-step temporal process, but if the actor is going to attempt any sort of self-evaluation, these two steps, for all practical purposes, must be condensed into one. Certainly during the later stages of rehearsals, the actor must create (the state of inspiration) and evaluate (the state of elaboration) at the same time. There is always a part of the actor that is deeply involved in the character, in the situation, in "the moment," as one says in the theater. But there is also another part of the actor that should be detached, monitoring his own work, sensing how the entire scene is going, receiving and processing perceptual cues from the audience. How this happens, how this division in the actor's mind develops—what might be called a split into a participating and observing self—will be discussed later.

The other major implication of the actor-as-instrument is that he uses himself in a total way; his primary tool is himself. Props, costumes, makeup, sets, lights, and sound effects are secondary tools that are not necessary components of a successful performance. Shakespeare's plays were originally performed in modern dress, without scenery, in broad daylight, with a minimum of props and sound effects. Figuratively speaking, his actors carried the visual elements on stage with them. Shakespeare appealed to the theater of the imagination, the theater inside the spectator's head. This is the way Alfred Harbage put it in his splendid book *Theatre for Shakespeare*.[1]

These visual elements can increase the entertainment value of a production and function as aids to the audience's "suspension of disbelief." But audiences are remarkably flexible in what they will or will not accept as true on the stage. Consider the swords in the final duel of *Hamlet*. Surely, the duel could not take place without them. But, in fact, it has. In one production, Hamlet's sword slipped out of his hands just as he had gotten hold of the poisoned, untipped rapier from Laertes. The sword was irretrievable; it had slid off stage. The actor transformed his entire arm into a rapierlike appendage (just as a child will transform his hand into a gun), using the index finger to represent the poisoned tip. The audience readily accepted this sudden, unprepared-for shift of convention. There was no uncomfortable shuffling, no laughter in response to a "mistake."

Indeed, the effect was quite startling: Hamlet's rigid rapier-arm became a physical metaphor for the final scene, where Hamlet himself had become an engine of destruction.

The secondary tools of the trade may reinforce the actor's sense of belief in the situation, but they cannot create it. In fact, they can interfere with an actor's work and often belie the illusion they have been called upon to reinforce. A prop is a meaningless object on stage until the actor has endowed it with meaning. Unless he believes in its reality, in its significance to the character, it has none for the audience. In *Death of a Salesman*, Biff, Willy Loman's son, discovers a piece of rubber tubing that his father has connected to the gas burner. Willy has thought of killing himself. During final rehearsals, the actor playing Biff had to do a great deal of work on his use of this simple object. At first, he held it without giving any attention to what he was holding; it was crushed in his hand; his face had very little expression on it. The actor was making the unwarranted assumption that simply because he had the object in his hand, all was well. But the moment was lifeless.

Only after the actor took the time to study the object—to feel its texture, study its shape and size, smell it, try to use it as his father might, in other words, to endow it with meaning—only then did his imagination begin to work. The moment changed. The rubber tube "came alive." It was held gently, carefully, lovingly; Biff's face registered great pain. He was holding his father's life in his hands. In its final transformation, the rubber tube came to represent Willy Loman's beating heart.

These same creative propositions can also hold true for costumes as well. Ralph Richardson was preparing for Falstaff. He had seen the costume sketches and knew that he would be provided with large amounts of body padding to create the picture of a very fat man. At the first rehearsal, the stage manager gave Richardson a mock set of padding, a vestlike affair, which he thought would help the actor. But Richardson refused it: "No! No! You see, first, I've got to feel fat inside."

We return, then, to the actor's *primary* instrument: himself. How does an actor use himself? How does the actor go about feeling "fat inside"? How does he transform "an empty space" into his mother's "closet" at Elsinore? What does an actor do when he prepares, builds a character, creates a role?

The basic premise of most contemporary acting is that if the imaginative preparation of a role has been successful, then its physical expression will naturally and more effectively follow. Physical expression includes vocal intonations and emphases, pauses in speaking, gestures, movements; in short, all those things that the audience can actually see and hear. But the actor's work proceeds, more often than not, from the inside out. After the inner foundation has been laid, the actor will then turn his attention to "the externals" of the role, perfecting and refining these manifestations of the internal imaginative state. Yet the rehearsal process of very experienced actors rarely follows such a rigid pattern. They are able to oscillate between the interior and exterior manifestations of character at will. It is never a question of "inside" first and then "outside."

Furthermore, the actor tries to avoid reproducing what he thinks an inner emotional state should look or sound like. "Acting has nothing to do with emotion" is the way I put it to first-year acting students, who invariably begin their training with the notion that acting is emotion. This notion is not held only by acting students; the average audience believes that acting is essentially to be equated with feeling. To the contrary, acting is behavior. *It is a complex process of doing things.* If the preparation has been correct, the emotion will be there when the actor needs it. To play at being angry can only lead to grimaces, posturing, and clichés.

Actors go out of their way to avoid such "result-playing," because there is a great temptation to skip the inner preparation and go right to the effect, for example, laughter, tears, irritation, disgust. But effects are only meaningful on stage when they are the result of an inner creative process. For instance, Actor D will avoid committing himself to line readings too early for fear that such a commitment will freeze the moment into a sterile cliché and cut off opportunities for further exploration. The same applies to his movements and gestures. He does this to compensate for his tendency to go directly to a big bravura effect, something which he is particularly adept at. At first readings of a play, Actor D will often carry this principle to the extreme. He will be so inaudible at times that he must look up from his script in order to let the other actors know when he has finished his speech so they can proceed with theirs. Early in his career D was often criticized for taking the easy, "effective" way out.

Parallel with the premise that external expression is mediated by inner processes is the idea that the words a character speaks are mainly the surface manifestations of inner, motivational states. "The text is an unimportant result of something else that's going on and it's our job to find out what that something else is." Michel Saint-Denis said this in his opening directorial remarks to the cast of *The Cherry Orchard*, which included Peggy Ashcroft, John Gielgud, Dorothy Tutin, Ian Holm, Roy Dotrice, and Judi Dench. Saint-Denis would never make this kind of statement with regard to Shakespeare, where the text is certainly not an unimportant result. But even in performing Shakespeare, the actor cannot fall into the trap of speaking as if he were reciting lines of poetry. Interior work has to be done on Shakespeare's text as well; images have to be supported by the imagination; the text represents the thoughts of the character. The work here, however, is much more complex.

The notion that the actor somehow has to get underneath the words usually leads him to question the text in a certain way: Who am I? Where am I? What do I want? Why do I want it? All these questions are related to the final question, How am I going to get it?[2] With very experienced actors, these questions are rarely posed in the methodical order that the following presentation might suggest. Gifted actors intuitively ask these kinds of questions of themselves all the time, but only when they are pressed to describe their technique do they reveal such processes of work as we are now about to look at.[3]

In the early stages of the work, "Who am I?" is answered as specifically as possible, based upon information found in the text. Answers such as "I am a cruel, ambitious, sadistic woman" are not acceptable; it is impossible to act "cruel" or "sadistic." These descriptive terms have a vantage point outside of the character and, although they might occur to an audience or literary critic, they are of little help to the actress. Worse still, they will probably prevent her from getting closer to the character, from seeing the variety in the woman, precisely because their vantage point is outside. But an answer such as the following is initially more helpful because it sticks to the facts and avoids value judgments: "I am thirty-five, the eldest of three daughters of the king, married to Albany, childless."

"Where am I?" refers to the specifics of location, not only the place but the entire sensory environment of "place": the temperature, the smells, the texture of the floor, the view from the window, the relationship of *this* place to the rest of the house, and so forth. Its answer comes from the text.

"What do I want?" usually comes from the text but needs to be supplemented by the actor's own invention. The question is not applied to the entire part. It is used in relation to separate, distinct sections or "units" of each scene in which the character appears. The actor breaks down a scene into such units, and a new unit is defined as a change in the "I want."

The answer to the question "What do I want?" is usually called an intention or an objective. The form in which the objective is stated, that is to say, the answer to the What question, can be very specific and concrete. A great many actors have found it useful to conceptualize this answer as a statement of a wish: "I want," followed by an active verb; for example, "I want to force him to stay," not, "I want him to stay in the room." *It is in the activity of the verb that the actor finds the things he will do in rehearsal.*

"Why do I want it?" often has to be invented by the actor or suggested by the situation (plot) or, to use the standard terminology, "the given circumstances." We shall have much more to say about this aspect of the actor's preparation later because it involves making the character's intentions or motivations so personal and so immediate that the actor eventually feels impelled to accomplish his objective at all costs.

The first four questions—Who? Where? What? Why?— are part of the actor's homework. But the How question can almost never be answered outside the rehearsal because the means of achieving the objective will depend upon what the other actor is doing during that particular rehearsal. How am I going to force him to stay in the room? can change from rehearsal to rehearsal. For example, one time "he" may be settled rather comfortably in his chair, drink in hand. In this case, I don't have to try very hard to force him; perhaps all I need do is give him my total attention. Another time, he may be looking anxiously toward the door, or be halfway to it. Now, I will have to find a more insistent way of accomplishing my objective, even if it means locking the door and hiding the key. It must be remembered that the other actor has got his own intentions to accomplish and it is out of the conflict between these potentially opposing objectives that the scene develops. This can even happen in performance. Harvey Keitel, appearing in David Rabe's *Hurlyburly*, observed, "There are some nights when a certain actor hits me, smacks me on my arm at a certain moment. Some nights he doesn't, and I react differently according to what he does. You multiply that by scores of things." And Judith Ivey, his partner, seconded him. "Things change on a nightly basis. We don't talk about it. It just happens on stage" (Bennetts 1984, p. C17).

The given circumstances of a play, or its situational elements, dictate the rules of the game for the actors, supplying a structure in rehearsals. In order to force someone to stay, an actress could, I suppose, use a gun, but such a choice would most probably be proscribed by the given circumstances. Actually, the scene I have in mind comes from *A Streetcar Named Desire*. Blanche wants to make Mitch, a potential beau, a desperately needed friend, stay with her. A gun is quite clearly out of the question; as a matter of fact, so is a locked door since one of the "givens" is that Stanley and Stella live in an apartment that has no locks. Blanche must find other ways to accomplish her objective. These other ways, these "activities" or "tasks," could include mixing him a drink, turning on the electric fan, offering to hang up his coat. Most important, the actress has Blanche's words at her disposal: tell him an interesting story, flatter him by inquiring about his life, show concern for his ailing mother, and so forth.

As is readily apparent, this way of working starts with the text, which is the initial source of inspiration for the actor, and then goes underground for a while. Finally, the actor returns to the text, which has now become enriched by his imaginative contribution. The gifted actor is able to do this without distorting the author's intentions or violating the basic meaning and form of the author's words. Interestingly enough, this approach, in its emphasis on playing out the actions, the verbs, the objectives as a means toward creating a character, recalls a famous passage from Aristotle's *Poetics*: "For tragedy is not an imitation of men but of actions and of life. It is in action that happiness and unhappiness are found, and the end we aim at is a kind of activity, not a quality. . . . It is not for the purpose of presenting their characters that the agents engage in action, but rather it is for the sake of their actions that they take on the characters they have" (Hutton translation, p. 51). In one sense, then, with regard to the creation of a character, the audience supplies the adjectives while the actors supply the verbs.

Personalization: In the Empathic Moment

An actor's preparation, then, begins with his search for the objective, the active verb. A character's role consists of a multitude of objectives but as rehearsals progress, the actor will revise some of his initial choices—condense some objectives and expand others. To the outsider this will appear as a shaping process. Furthermore, as the actor becomes more familiar with the sequence of objectives and the given circumstances, he begins to discern what Stanislavski called the "through-line-of-action." If we imagine this through-line to be the spine of the role, then each single objective is one vertebra. Discovering the spine prevents a character from existing only in "bits and pieces," and later it permits the actor to live a continuous life-as-the-character on stage during performance. As F. Scott Fitzgerald remarked in *The Great Gatsby*, "Personality is an unbroken series of successful gestures."

The actor's work on himself, however, cannot stop here. After he has isolated a particular objective, he must find a way to make it meaningful to himself, meaningful in the sense of intensifying his total belief in the necessity of accomplishing it. He must "justify" it; he must "personalize" it. This is the actor's way of establishing empathy with his character. As we have already seen, an actor has to bring life to a prop he is using. In an analogous way, having found a playable objective, one that coincides with the author's intentions, the actor cannot take *it* for granted either; he must make it come alive for himself. Answering the questions What do I want? and Why do I want it? is not enough. The actor must now make these answers so important to himself, so vital and immediate in his imagination, that he is compelled toward action.

There is more controversy surrounding this issue of personalization than almost any other in the theater. Part of it is based on a confusion between the idea of personalization and what Stanislavski referred to as "emotion memory." While it is not within the scope of this book to discuss the matter in detail, it is necessary to outline it to some degree because personalization, a profound empathy with the character, is a central element in the preparation of every gifted actor. It is ultimately the key to the fullest possible transformation of oneself into a character. Needless to say, some actors never have to give it a name; miraculously, it is there for them when they seem to need it.

Stanislavski (1936) said, "Always and forever, when you are on stage, you must play yourself. But it will be in an infinite variety of combinations of objectives and given circumstances which you have prepared for your part and which have been smelted in the furnace of your emotion memory" (p. 167). "Emotion memory" refers to a technique of recalling incidents from one's past "which makes you relive the sensations you once felt" (p. 158). Actors are trained to revive both the affective and the ideational components of a memory. Today, however, "emotion memory" is not taken to mean that the actor must engage in substitutions of his own past for the moment-to-moment life of the character's present. Emotion memory exercises (affective memory as it is now called) are seen as part of the actor's work on himself and not necessarily in relation to a specific role. (For a full discussion of this issue, see Wiles 1980, pp. 13–36.)

Nevertheless, some actors will explain that their route to personalization can involve finding similar situations in their own lives, exploring such situations in detail, recalling them to memory and using this experiential data to justify a particular objective or event in the play. The problem here is obvious. By using the memories of past events in one's life to create an emotionally charged objective, the actor is in danger of scaling the character down to his size. This becomes particularly evident, say, in Shakespeare, but the danger applies to Chekhov as well. For example, an actor was having difficulty in connecting with Macbeth's deepest wishes to obtain the crown. During rehearsals, he managed to reactivate early memories of desperately wanting a special toy at Christmas. He then attempted to use this as a substitute for Macbeth's wish for the crown in order to make the part come alive inside him. The end result, of course, was a Macbeth who appeared childish, petulant, and whiney—a Macbeth incapable of projecting the dimensions of suffering demanded by Shakespeare's text.

Other actors, however, are more careful in both their understanding of and their use of such revivals of the past. For example, Laurence Olivier, preparing the famous cry of pain for the blinded Oedipus's last entrance, explained that "most of us need secondary images to support this sort of intensity of expression." He thought about "the ermine that is trapped by salt scattered upon the hard snow. This ermine starts to lick, but the cunning mixture holds fast to its tongue, keeping it prisoner though it tries to tear itself free. Trading upon this animal torment helped me to produce a horrifying enough noise. It is, as has been said, next to impossible to produce the effect of great suffering unless the actor endures some degree of it" (1982, p. 145).

Still others make use of themselves in extremely personal and private ways without recourse to specific memories from their pasts, using instead what Stanislavski called "the creative if": if I were in his shoes, what would I do? Stanislavski emphasized the conditional aspect of this proposition because it virtually catapults the actor into the character's position, demanding an imaginative transformation of one's own self-image. Donald Pleasence said, "There comes a moment on-stage when you can't deny yourself and you can't deny the part you are playing. Somehow these two things come together when you act" (Ross and Ross 1962, p. 256). Peter Hall, directing Albert Finney in the role of Hamlet, visited him during an intermission of the dress rehearsal. Finney "sat there covered in sweat crying his eyes out. He cried and cried and cried. I asked him if he would like me to go. No, he said, he felt he'd unblocked something in himself. What we'd had before was energy, ferocity, and agility. What we had tonight was a man exposing his own heart" (1984, p. 235).

Successful actors who are in a position to reject offers say that the initial decision to do a role is based, in part, upon some intuitive awareness of their capability of personalizing the character. From a psychological standpoint, we are in the realm of potential identifications. Wittels (1939) called these "the phantoms of the actor." Leavy, although he was referring to the poet Keats, described a process that is equally applicable to the actor: he must enter into "transient but intense fusions with his images in the empathic moment" (1970, p. 214). Access to a wide range of conscious, but more important, unconscious images of the self and others will permit an actor greater variety in his choice of role. But more of this later.

Finally, there are some actors, unlike Pleasence, who won't even talk about personalization. One such actor, playfully suspicious of his director's "Method" inclinations, said to him, "Tell me what you want; give me a few days and I'll give it to you. But don't ever, *ever* ask me how I did it. That's my secret!"

Personalization also applies to a character's occupation or over-all life situation. Marlon Brando worked out in Stillman's gym for three months in preparation for the part of an ex–prize fighter in *On the Waterfront*. Rip Torn apprenticed as an assistant chef (to the dismay of some customers) in a New York restaurant in order to personalize the experience for Arnold Wesker's *The Kitchen*. And Actress A, during rehearsals in which she played a recently divorced housewife, watched Cassavetes's film *Husbands* as if she were the character from the play. This actress, in fact, will often perform her usual early morning tasks (breakfast, shower, dressing) as if it were the character doing these things.

But there is yet another aspect of personalization which deserves special attention. In the *Streetcar* scene between Blanche and Mitch, the actress had defined one of her objectives as "I want to force him to stay." Addressing ourselves to the "I" and the "him" in this proposition, a new issue arises, namely, in early rehearsals, who is the "I," who is the "him"? The actress's activities in the scene must be based upon what the other actor is actually doing in the rehearsal. The actress will not be working honestly if she rehearses the scene as if the other actor were doing what she thought he should do. In this case, the actress would really be playing both parts to the detriment of her spontaneity and sense of truth. This is another variation of "result-playing."

For better or worse, her Mitch is the other actor in the room, the other *real* person, and not some imaginary idea of how Mitch should look, sound, or behave. A rehearsal begins with two real people facing each other; actors monitor and use their own responses toward each other. Inevitably, the actress has certain feelings, thoughts, and attitudes about the actor, and she may find *within them* a valid reason to force him to stay. She may, for instance, notice that he has a pleasant smile, or that he wears a particularly nice after-shave lotion, or that the sound of his voice is soothing to her, or (and this would be very helpful for the scene) that he is to some degree sexually exciting in her eyes. In a similar scene from another play, all the actress could find to work with at first was the fact that "he," in reality, was a world famous star, and she wanted to make him stay in order to preserve the thrill of being in his presence.

Fundamentally, Actress B, not yet Blanche, confronts Actor M, not yet Mitch. Actress B's attention is focused on Actor M, who becomes the target of her objective. In her reactions to Actor M, she tries to find the answer to the Why question, her justification, her personalization. But as the work continues into the middle stages, inner transforma-

tions in Actor M begin to take place; they manifest themselves as a series of identifiable, recognizable patterns of
behavior which Actress B can more readily accept as Mitch.
Of course, a complementary process is taking place within
Actress B so that the transformations she recognizes in
Actor M only help her to reinforce a growing belief in her
own Blanche.

The creation of a character can never really be accomplished in isolation; the actor's imagination is stimulated by
the ways in which the other actor-character relates to him.
For this reason Actor D without being falsely modest can
attribute "60 percent of the success of my performance to
the person I'm playing the scene with." Christopher
Walken agrees. "Everything is a collaboration. It's very
hard to say who did what, because we've all given to and
stolen from each other so much" (Bennetts 1984, p. C17).

One final point must be made: actors take nothing for
granted. We have seen how they avoid setting a line reading or a gesture; they do not take the externals of a role for
granted. Even though I know from the text that Mitch is
going to leave, I still must play my own objective as strongly
as possible. It is Mitch's job to leave; I must not do the
leaving for him. Taking nothing for granted, in other
words, also means dealing with what is actually there in the
rehearsal hall and not with what one thinks should be there,
not with an already created Mitch.

Actor M is wearing a red tie today: Ok! Mitch is wearing a
red tie. It happens to be raining in New York City today: Ok!
It's raining in New Orleans. I had a bit too much to drink last
night: ergo, Blanche has a mild hangover this morning. The
rehearsal proceeds on these premises. Tomorrow, they may
be different. These experimental interactions can only take
place—without violating the truth and spontaneity of the
moment—if the actors willingly accept the givens of the
moment and take nothing for granted. It is in this sense that
the actor makes total use of himself, that his primary instrument is himself.

In rehearsal the actor's attention is not focused primarily
on himself but on the other player. Or, to put it more
precisely, his attention oscillates between the external

stimuli and his inner responses to them. John Houseman, directing Maureen Stapleton, reported his experience with a certain amount of awe. "At first, I didn't know what the hell she was doing. She's marvelous! She was all ears, all antennae, wandering about the room, searching, searching, exploring. She was letting Jason [Robards] do the work for her." Actress A couldn't remember what she had done that the director liked so much not only because her work had vanished the moment she stopped rehearsing. She couldn't remember because she wasn't ready to. She was still in that early stage of work when her total concentration was on her partners and on the inner life of the character. Because she was so engrossed in her own imagination, she needed the director to reflect back to her whatever external manifestations of her work had begun to show.

In early rehearsals, the external expression of the role is almost irrelevant to the actor. Irrelevant to the actor but not to the director; if he should feel that an actor's work has taken too private a turn, he will steer the actor in a different direction. The marvel of watching gifted actors rehearse is that, while they are engaged in this very personal process of exploration, their voices and bodies remain astonishingly responsive to and expressive of even the most subtle inner signals. This has led many visitors at rehearsals to conclude that British actors work in a totally different way from Americans, but the fact is that the imaginative work is essentially the same.

Therefore, what the actor tries to repeat or practice are the inner objectives of the character and not the vocal intonations or physical gestures. And what the actor remembers in early rehearsals is often isolated and fragmented: sensory stimuli (the red tie, the rain, the headache); the successful accomplishment of an objective; or, more likely, in the face of failure to fulfill the objective, a hunch as to how to go about it next time. In an attempt to evaluate their own work actors will say, "It felt right. I don't know why yet, but it felt right." Here the actor could mean that he felt connected with his partner or that he felt somehow connected inside: organic, resonant. Probably, the "I want" he was pursuing linked up with some personally acceptable self-image. But in those instances where a director says he likes it and the actor protests that it was not any good at all, the opposite has probably occurred: the "I want" linked up with an undesirable, ego-alien self-image, that is to say, the "I want" touched upon certain systems of unconscious wishes within the actor that he, for a variety of reasons, finds unacceptable.

So far we have been considering the implications of the fact that the actor is his own instrument. His product vanishes from reality the moment he stops working. Moreover, the actor initially is not concerned so much with externals; his attention is focused alternatively on the inner imaginative life of the character (the objectives) and on the behavior of his partners. A rehearsal is the place for controlled experimentation and research, a time to try out any and all ideas and impulses within the framework of the given circumstances. Rehearsals are the place to make mistakes, and actors often find out what's right by intentionally doing something that's wrong. "On the stage, you have to find the truth, even if you have to lose the audience" is the epigrammatic way in which Anthony Quinn says the same thing (Ross and Ross 1962, p. 373).

This is a state of affairs, in other words, where the actor's self-observing and self-critical mechanisms are compromised by the very nature of his craft. He must be able to tolerate a great deal of ambiguity in his work and possess to some extent that quality which Keats called "Negative Capability, that is when man is capable of being in uncertainties, Mysteries, doubts, without any irritable reaching after fact and reason" (Leavy 1970, p. 201). If all he can say about his work is that "it felt right," then the actor has to find some way out of this dilemma of uncertainty in order to prepare for the eventual and inevitable public performance. He is forced to find some reliable mirror.

2

PRIVATE TO PUBLIC

Acting is easy. All you gotta do is get out on stage, talk loud, and
don't hit the furniture.

—George Abbott

"I want to get help"

Fortunately for the actor, he is not working alone. The
theater is a collaborative art form, and the actor's most
important ally and companion, his reliable mirror, is the
stage director.

The director as we know him today is a relatively new
phenomenon in the theater. Prior to the twentieth century,
stage managers supervised the integration of the various
elements of a production but not in any creative sense, not
with a particular concept of the play in mind. They simply
brought together all the elements of the show on time and in
good working condition. The actor-manager emerged a bit
later, taking over some of the functions of the stage manager, while enlarging in significant ways his part in the
production process. The actor-manager edited the text to
make the entire play more attractive to the audience's
tastes, often to exhibit his own talents in a better light, "to
fatten up the part" by cutting out extraneous characters and
reshaping the structure of scenes. Because the basic
assumptions we make today about acting, not to mention
the conditions of theatrical performance, are so different,

the actor-manager's function with regard his fellow troupers' acting was undoubtedly limited.[1] Furthermore, even the idea that an actor needed to receive formal training was a relatively late phenomenon. When the American Academy of Dramatic Arts opened its doors in 1884, this was considered to be so unusual that it made front-page news.

The theater was essentially presentational in form and highly conventionalized—presentational in the sense that it acknowledged the existence of the audience as one of its main conventions. This radically affected the assumptions that both audience and actors made about their respective roles in the theatrical event. Audiences' expectations were quite different, especially with regard to the actor's presentation of identifiable, recognizable aspects of human behavior. The presentational theater did not necessarily demand realism from its performers. Actually, the theater could not demand realism as we know it when, for instance, the audience sat on stage. One night David Garrick had to fight off a drunken spectator who was fondling an actress's breasts during a scene (Sheldon 1967, p. 71).

Representational drama made its appearance in the late nineteenth century. This is sometimes referred to as the theater of the "fourth wall." The presence of the audience is no longer overtly acknowledged; they are looking at the action of the play through an imaginary fourth wall. The growth of representational drama was quickened by the work of Stanislavski and André Antoine, among others, whose theories about acting were predominantly psychological. Highly conventionalized acting gave way to psychological realism at a time when the modern sensibilities of playwrights as different as Chekhov, Ibsen, Strindberg, and Pirandello demanded it.

Psychological naturalism bred and nourished the growth of the contemporary director. While his prototype, the actor-manager, certainly interpreted the text, he did so more in a literary sense, an *explication du texte*. The director of today not only performs this function, but he also makes a series of interventions, aimed at the actor, designed to uncover that "something else" of which "the text is an unimportant result."

In what follows, "the director" is a construct created for this book; it is based upon the ways in which scores of different directors work. Just as most experienced actors intuitively respond to rehearsals, rarely thinking in terms of the Who, Where, What, Why questions, so, too, gifted directors behave and respond spontaneously. This composite picture is meant to highlight certain similarities in technique to which most directors aspire.

Based upon past experiences with directors, the actor enters into this relationship with certain preformed assumptions about what is to be demanded of him and what he can rightfully expect from the director. In other words, even before the first rehearsal begins, a contract exists, usually implicit and unstated, between these two parties. From the actor's standpoint, one could say that it takes the following form: *I want to get help from the director.*[2]

During rehearsals, the conscious and unconscious meanings of the verb (to get), the object (help) and, most important, the indirect object (the director) undergo significant changes. For instance, *help* often undergoes a series of transformations as follows: "help"—knowledge, advice, encouragement, criticism, approval, attention, security, warmth, a smile, a glance, a hug, a kiss, in effect, love. *To get* can change as the intensity of the need increases: "want to get"—must have, demand, steal, seduce. But the change in *the director*, that is to say, his image in the actor's mind, is mainly an unconscious one: he becomes an obscure object of the actor's desire for help. The director temporarily comes to represent significant figures in the actor's life, in particular, mother and father. These changes can also be expressed by their negatives: "I want help" will sometimes be represented by its opposite, "I won't accept help from him." Furthermore, this schematic presentation is not meant to imply that such changes take place in this order or for that matter that they are irreversible. They are also not mutually exclusive: "I want advice" can coexist with "I want a hug," where the former might be conscious and the latter unconscious.

Actors are often unaware of the extent of their dependency needs; they have to deny them in order to preserve a sense of their own autonomy and that of the character they are creating (see p. 112). Some experienced actors seem to treat the director as nothing more than a stage manager, but appearances are deceptive. When such actors are urged to talk about their inner experience of rehearsals, when they are asked to give free rein to their thoughts about the director (an informal free association), one begins to see that the inner image of the director often does not match his outward form.

While the actor usually admits to himself that he needs the director's eye to a certain extent throughout rehearsals, he is unaware of the ramifications of this kind of working alliance. Functions that one normally performs for oneself—memory, perception, attention, reality-testing, self-criticism, control of tension derived from repressed wishes demanding to be satisfied—such functions are partially taken over by the director during the rehearsal of a scene. At the unconscious, and sometimes conscious or preconscious, level the actor has entrusted to his director his self-appraising system, and the implications of this transfer can be quite profound indeed.[3]

The director, by his attitude and approach to the work, reinforces the actor's initial assumptions about the help he will offer. For instance, directors consider it their job to create the proper working atmosphere in which the actor can grow into his character. The director tries to establish a sense of freedom to explore, to investigate, even to fail.

Along these lines, the director may initially avoid right-wrong, good-bad statements. He is only interested in human behavior and yet "interested" is not quite the right word, for the actor is under no obligation to be "interesting." This would tend to push the actor toward result-playing. Furthermore, the actor cannot be permitted to become a carbon copy of the director by unintentionally assuming his mannerisms, vocal intonations, and so forth. Therefore, most directors try to avoid giving line readings or showing an actor how to make a gesture too early in the rehearsal process.

Directors may not use verbal interventions at all; by indirections they find direction out. This approach is effectively, if rather dramatically, illustrated by the following example from a play which dealt with fifteen men in prison, all hard-core criminals. Although homosexuality was not the main theme of the play—loyalty and self-determination were—many of the characters clearly were homosexual. This was an essential element to embed within the perform-ances, but difficult to accomplish because there were no textual references to it of any kind. The homosexuality was an implicit given, just like the cramped quarters, the poor food, and the inevitable day of execution for some. But the director felt that to make direct references to the erotic would have thrown the production out of focus.

The solution arrived at was to ask the actors to rehearse in the nude for the first two days. They were prohibited from paying any (conscious) attention to this rather remark-able adjustment in rehearsal practice. It was business as usual: the exploration of objectives. Beginning with the third rehearsal, the actors were asked to bring in one piece of clothing a day, which then became a permanent part of their costume: Actor E first wore a jockstrap, Actor F a white athletic sock, and Actor H a colored bandanna. It took about ten days before the actors were fully clothed.

This device proved effective. The memory of these early rehearsals remained alive in the actors' imaginations. No verbal statements had to be made about the homosexual underplot. The impact of seeing the naked, male body was apparently enough.[4] Without any overt intervention on the director's part, a palpable atmosphere of paranoia and jealousy had been generated. The paranoia was explicit in the text and absolutely necessary for the play; the jealousy, never referred to in dialogue, was equally necessary to justify the final set of murders.

I do not wish to give the impression that this is a common occurrence. I have chosen this extreme example of how a director can adjust the working atmosphere to dramatize my point. Most directors work in subtle, often quiet ways, yet the more usual events in rehearsal are not qualitatively different from this.

The Rehearsing-Actor

The opening phase of rehearsal usually begins with several readings of the play, followed by an analysis of each scene.[5]

The actor has begun his own script breakdown, and he may have made tentative notations in his script concerning the objectives he wants to investigate. The cast and director agree on the external requirements of place, the socioeconomic status of the characters, pertinent historical data, and so forth. The actor begins testing out and clarifying his objectives with his colleagues. On the other hand, while attempting to answer the "How am I going to get it" question, he may revise his understanding of the character's intentions. The text is usually studied in bits and pieces; the work is frequently interrupted by any member of the cast or the director. This phase has a stop-start rhythm to it. Indeed, once the director begins to organize parts of scenes into sections of an act, we know we have entered the middle-rehearsal phase.

Flexibility is the hallmark of this phase of the work. Because each play poses different rehearsal problems, there is bound to be a great variety in directorial approach to these opening days.

Several examples may help to indicate the range of this flexibility. First, scenes are not necessarily studied in order. The structure of the play, the pattern in which the characters come and go, the tempo in which conflicts develop and resolve themselves suggest different rehearsal strategies. Second, not all scenes are given the same relative amount of rehearsal time. The texture of a scene, its dramatic density, the demands it makes on the actors' state of personalization of the characters, the quality and intensity of the conflict— all these factors influence the director's decisions about time allocation. An extremely daring example occurred when Director C spent three weeks working only on the first five pages of the script. One and a half weeks were allotted to the remaining one hundred and fifteen pages. Director C was then at the peak of his career. It is doubtful if another, less prominent director could control the anxiety generated by such a tactic.

Finally, directors can minimize their activity during this phase in order to encourage the actors' total freedom to explore. During rehearsals of a particularly abstruse play, in which the actors' initial, spontaneous, deeply personal responses to the text were going to be crucial indicators of how they would have to be guided in later rehearsals, the director said absolutely nothing to them for the first four days. The actors walked through the entire play, moving wherever they wanted to, doing whatever came to mind, censoring nothing. Rehearsals started each day with "Ok, let's begin" and ended with "We'll stop here for today." After watching for four days, the director felt he was in a good position to help the actors select and order their objectives, which had become increasingly clear throughout these nonstructured rehearsals. The text gave no clues whatsoever to motivation; all this had to come from the actors' imaginations. Jean Vilar at the Théâtre National Populaire often used to rehearse his repertory company this way.[6]

At the same time that he tries to create an appropriate rehearsal atmosphere, the director is getting to know each actor's unique way of working. He begins to understand what specific help the actor will require, that is to say, what type of stimuli from the environment will best activate the actor's imagination. A significant way in which the director adjusts the working alliance is by controlling his closeness to the actor. Many directors will stand next to an actor as he plays out a scene, whispering into his ear, speaking partly to him and partly to his character, addressing him by the character's name. It is only in the middle phase that the director will move farther away from the actor, but, even here, it is a separation of no more than 10 to 15 feet.

Some actors cannot bear a great deal of intimacy, nor do they necessarily need it. The director's interventions will proceed all the way from silence, on the one hand, to overt support, on the other ("Yes!! Yes!! Wonderful!!). Other kinds of statements directors make to their actors take the following forms: "You know, you're probably going to have to try something else, stronger, more effective, to force him to stay." Or, "It occurs to me that Claudius may be going on so long *because* he wants to keep Hamlet quiet." "Do you really want that cup of coffee? Or is it more a means to an end?" And, of course, when actors present ideas of their own, most directors are receptive.

The director can also begin to predict trouble spots. For example, he estimates whether private work with a particular actor will be necessary. He is alert to the actor's tendency to intellectualize as a means of avoiding the emotional work. Thinking too much, instead of doing, needs to be combatted continuously. "What do you think of my idea of Mitch's mother-fixation?" received a half-joking response, aimed simply at getting this actor to reorient his point of view away from that of "spectator–literary critic *cum* psychologist." His work in the scene betrayed the fact that he was playing an idea instead of a person. The director also mediates among actors as he sees conflicts develop, referring back to a possible misunderstanding of the text, the given circumstances, or the initial objectives.

During the opening phase, actors often try to impress the director or to control him. The actor is still struggling with his fantasies of the director as the authoritarian casting figure who had to be pleased, placated, or held at bay. A need to control can also be focused on the other members of the company. In both instances, it represents ways in which the actor copes with the newness and the strangeness of the situation. For instance, Actor D, we recall, is sometimes barely audible at first readings. At a conscious level he justifies this behavior by maintaining that it avoids result-playing. At an unconscious level, its function is to control the other actors and it also represents his (pre-)conscious wish "to run away and hide."

The transition into the middle phase is signaled by the bringing together of bits and pieces of scenes into a larger whole. This phase, unlike the opening, has a rather clearly defined end point: the first, uninterrupted run-through of the entire play. While flexibility of approach characterizes the opening phase, a more consistent pattern now becomes evident. In a systematic way, sections of each act are assembled in their playing order to give the cast a chance to solidify and reinforce their discoveries about the characters. A deepening of the work occurs (the personalization). Continuity of acting is stressed.

The most apparent difference between the opening and middle phase is that there are now significantly fewer interruptions. The actor tries to let the scene play through; the director resists the temptation to stop. This is not an easy task for either party. The opening phase, with its playfulness, its complete freedom to try anything, its manifest lack of structure, is intensely pleasurable. But the middle phase brings with it certain limitations to the actor's behavior.

The staging is now set. Movements and gestures, which the actor had made spontaneously now have to be coordinated and mediated by the director's eye. Furthermore, the actor can no longer linger over a moment to explore its deeper implications; he is forced to move on to the next objective, even though he senses that the previous one has not "felt right." He must develop his through-line of action. In addition, he no longer has the latitude to improvise with his partners: the written text becomes more important, and stage movement, under the director's guidance, has to reflect the underlying rhythm and structure of the scene.

The learning of lines has also become a necessity since the actor wants to keep the scene moving forward. As he becomes clearer about his objectives, the actor usually finds that the author's words quite naturally come to mind as the best, the most precise, often the most eloquent external expression of his inner needs. Sometimes, one can get valuable clues about an actor's development in a part from those instances where he forgets a line or substitutes his own word for the text word. Exploration of such slips can even take one to preconscious determinants. Actor B kept saying "To be or not to be—that is the point!" This version of the world's most famous line actually appears in the First Quarto of the play, considered by Shakespeare scholars as the "Bad Quarto." Actor B, a scholar in his own right, knew this, too. His mischievous slip represented his own fears about doing the part as well as a condemnation of his own rehearsal work. He told me that in some way he knew he was doing the "bad Hamlet."

The actor now tries to come to terms with personalizing the role, making it his own. His homework becomes as important to him as his rehearsal work; he needs privacy to accomplish what is essentially a task of introspection. The work takes on an obsessional cast. Thoughts of his director and of the rehearsals are continually on his mind. For example, the husband of a distinguished actress had to move into a hotel during this phase of the work in order, so he thought, to protect their marriage. He was faced with his wife's inability (or, perhaps, appropriate unwillingness) to lose touch with the character she was creating and the director who was guiding her. She had invested her role and her director with such large amounts of psychic energy that she had little left over for other love relations. Her husband experienced this rejection as a narcissistic blow and he replied in kind.

Through "personalization" the director attempts to help the actor unlock the door to his subconscious, as Stanislavski put it (1936), in order to build the character. The director can only facilitate this process. The actor has to do the "growing" himself, and he makes use of all the data he has gathered, such as his perceptions of the outer world of the play and the inner world of his character's intentions, to aid him in this task. The crucial operative questions are still What do I want? and Why do I want it? but the accent has shifted from the interrogatives to the subject: what do *I* understand about this person's needs that can help me justify his actions to myself.

We have already come across examples of this process. The actor who was trying to bring "life" to the prop, the rubber hose, was involved in "personalizing" it. He permitted himself to have very intimate, painful thoughts and feelings about his own father and then found a way to relate them to the imaginative circumstances of the play. The actress who went to the films as if she were the character was doing the same thing. When she returned to her apartment, she recalled her own divorce and the absence of her son (at college). As the silence and the emptiness of her living room seemed to overwhelm her, she remembered how she felt when learning about the unexpected death of her brother. But behind these memories existed yet another configuration of images which, when she came upon them, astonished her. The actress had forgotten that for one year she had cared for her terminally ill father. It was only then that the full impact of the Cassavetes film *Husbands* dawned on her.

Creating a role demands that the actor assume new and temporary patterns of behavior, thought, and feeling, but the process is more than copying or imitating others: personalization is different from impersonation. Getting "deeper into the role" means that the actor is getting in touch with a variety of early, and often unconscious images of the self in relationship to others and these images carry with them their own affective charges. The actor will ultimately reorganize and reintegrate them into a new performing self which comes to represent the character that the actor will portray.

The director now begins to push the actors toward more autonomy by interrupting less, distancing himself physically, generally remaining still. The director recognizes that this phase of the work is very demanding; in a firm manner, he helps the actor resist the temptation to return to an earlier mode of work. Playfulness and the remarkable esprit of the opening phase is often replaced by petty bickering, apparent confusion about issues which had been clearly resolved just a few days earlier. There is also a marked increase in the actor's demands on the director's time. This sudden change in mood is fundamentally caused by the intrapsychic pressure of personalization and the implications of the director's distancing maneuvers.

Late night telephone calls to the director may begin; there is often a "hidden agenda." The actor is presumably calling about an unresolved rehearsal issue but, rather quickly, the conversation changes and the actor complains about his wife's distant behavior. This actor was also concerned about the distance he now felt from the director. Often, the issue comes up more directly: "I'm not getting enough direction. Why are you leaving me on my own?" This give-me-more actor is usually excessively alert to how much time the director spends with other actors. It seems to Actor D, for example, that his director has secrets to share with the favored few. The give-me-more also represented for this actor a "Let me in, too!" Actually, Actor D wanted nothing more than an arm around his shoulder to allay his separation fears. George S. Kaufman was apparently quite adept at handling give-me-more. He was once assailed by an actor who had received almost no direction at all during rehearsals: "Please, Mr. Kaufman, please just simply tell me how to play the part." Kaufman replied, "Under an assumed name."

The director also begins to intensify his interventions.

Direct confrontations become more frequent, questions re-
cede, and interpretations are aimed at a deeper level. A
direct confrontation holds "the mirror up to nature" and in
effect says, "Wait a minute. Look at what you're doing."
Implicit in such confrontations is the word "no." The director disagrees with what the actor is doing; there's something wrong. Confrontations, therefore, are usually han-
dled with tact so that the actor's autonomy is not limited any
more than is absolutely necessary.[7]

Director C, whom we will meet again a bit later, interrupted a run-through of *Streetcar Named Desire*. Stella,
having fled to her neighbors after Stanley's drunken and
violent outburst, is persuaded to return to him. Stanley,
standing at the bottom of the stairs, yells "with heaven-
splitting violence, '*STELL-LAHHHHH!*' [The stage direction continues:] The door upstairs opens again. Stella slips
down the rickety stairs in a robe. Her eyes are glistening
with tears. They stare at each other. Then they come
together with low, animal moans. He falls to his knees on
the steps and presses his face to her belly . . . Her eyes go
blind with tenderness" (Williams 1947, p. 66).

As the actress descended the stairs, the director charged
from his seat, shouting "No! No! No!—Stella! When you're
coming down, what do you *want*? Huh?" "Well, I'm thinking of how much I need Stanley, how much I want him,
how much I want to hold him." "No! No! No! There's only
one thing going through your mind—only one thing. Penis!
Penis! Penis! Now, go up and do the scene again."

Such an interpretation could have been improper in an
earlier phase, not because it was wrong, but because it
would have been premature, tactless, possibly offensive.
The actress would not have known what to do with it. Her
less loaded objective, her more surface intention, "I want to
hold him," permitted her, in the opening phase, to work
within the framework of a relatively nonconflicted, acceptable wish. The character's deeper wish, that is, for his
penis, if verbalized too early, would probably have frightened the actress and forced her to erect defenses against this
movement. Only when a real relationship, one of mutual
trust, had developed between the actors, could Director C
hazard the overt, sexual-anatomical interpretation.[8]

A final example illustrates how close a director may have to get to an actor in order to help resolve a serious impasse. Directors often have the opportunity of working with the same actor in many different plays. In fact, they look forward to working with actors whom they can trust and whose approach to acting is similar to theirs. Such was the case with Actor G and his director. However, the actor was having an inordinate amount of trouble with the part. After two weeks, both actor and director were contemplating defeat, that is, hiring someone else to play the part. This alternative was not attractive to the director although Actor G seemed inappropriately in favor of it.

The director suggested that Actor G move in with him until the play opened. He told the actor that this would give them more time to discuss the part. They could, as it were, rehearse day and night. They could "live through" the experience together. But the director told me that something else was going on. He had intuitively understood that Actor G, who was extremely narcissistic, was so resentful of the time the director spent with the other actors that G's work was suffering. Furthermore, G was a loner: he had very few friends and had experienced the rupture of several painful love affairs, which deepened his sense of worthlessness. In short, both G's work life and his private life left him feeling bereft. Staying with the director, as a guest in his house, offered G a temporary means of coping with these intensely painful issues. G's opening night performance was triumphant. However, the actor experienced more stage fright than ever before. The actor had managed to achieve a very deep transformation of self into character while, in the process of doing so, he had grown too close to his director and had to suffer the pain of separation. As we will see, the combination of these two factors plays a central role in the stage fright attack.

In short, the director tries to explain things to an actor when he, the actor, is able to hear them. A premature explanation can cause bewilderment at best; more likely, it will create an anxiety and avoidance which must be overcome by even greater effort. Finally, while most actors never have to get as close as Actor G did to his director, strong feelings of intimacy between the two inevitably de-

velop as the director guides the actor toward a deeper
personalization of the character's needs.

The actor, then, experiences this middle phase of rehearsals as one in which things are being taken away from
him; he must give up certain pleasurable and protecting
modes of behavior. Some of his own inhibitions and defenses must be overcome in the process of personalization.
Moreover, his freedom to play has now been restricted. He
has to memorize his words. However, there is a confusing
aspect to this phase of the work. Sometimes the director
seems to be very close to him; at other times, the director
seems to be moving away from him, ever so slightly changing his role in rehearsals from companion-collaborator to
spectator. And he hears the director's voice less often.

The first run-through both ends the middle phase and
signals the start of the final stage of the work which will
include several more run-throughs, technical rehearsals,
and dress rehearsals. The run-throughs still take place in
the rehearsal hall; with the "first tech," the company moves
into the theater.

Actors generally look forward to the first run-through.
The problems which initiated the middle phase seem to
have been resolved; the original esprit of the company has
returned; there is now a sense of pulling together toward a
common goal. This run-through poses a stimulating creative challenge for the actor. At last, something is going to
be put together. This will be his first opportunity to "exist"
on stage as the character. Becoming gives way to being;
analysis and fragmentation to synthesis and wholeness.
Technically, the actor must begin to forget about objectives,
given circumstances, adjustments, justifications. He must
dare to believe that the rehearsal work has been internalized
to such an extent that the stimuli from his own imagination
and from the other actors will elicit, spontaneously and
naturally, responses appropriate to his character. The
mechanics of preparation must now be hidden so that the
performance of the play can appear to be unrehearsed.[9]

During the first run-through, actors find that they discover many new things about their characters. Moments,
which had seemed obscure, had "felt wrong," suddenly are
infused with vitality and purpose. There is often a sense of

mystery about this process but its explanation is not hard to find. Certain passages in a play cannot "fit in" when rehearsed in the fragmented manner of the opening phase. Their *acting sense* only manifests itself when the units preceding and following them are fully played out. This is the essence of the through-line-of-action. Furthermore, inner resistances to deeper personalization may have been resolved outside the actor's awareness. In the first run-through, for example, an actor may come back to a scene which he has not rehearsed for a week. In the interim, while solving problems related to other passages in the play or deepening his imaginative understanding of a particular aspect of the character, the actor has unconsciously clarified these obscure moments.

The inner experience of a first run-through is one of excitement and pleasure. Something now exists in its entirety; a first draft, perhaps, which only awaits skillful editing. The actor feels swept along by the events of the play. Emotions begin to be there when he needs them; emphasis, phrasing, tempo seem to take care of themselves. The actor is not consciously making something happen ("indicating"); effortlessly, the character starts to take over. During intermissions, actors can be heard exchanging compliments: "That thing you did in our scene. It was marvelous. It helped me so much. Where did it come from?"[10]

Where, indeed, did it come from? This "high" does not last long. As run-throughs progress, the actor has trouble repeating things. New uncertainties arise because of the apparent randomness of each subsequent rehearsal. A scene that worked the first time and then "died" the second will inexplicably regain its vitality the fourth time through. Now the common complaint is "I wish we had more time." Rehearsals appear to have been rushed; the director was pushing too hard; he wanted results too quickly; we didn't have enough time to explore. In actuality, rehearsals do take place in a relatively short amount of time: about four weeks. But it is not real time the actor refers to; it is his subjective sense of time. His complaints are more often than not an expression of a wish to put off the opening night as far as possible. Just as the actor resists being pushed into the less flexible structure of the middle phase, he now resists what is clearly the final push. Once again, he wants to return to the honeymoon of the opening days of work with its sense of timelessness. This wish to stay in rehearsal also emerges during performance (see pp. 112–15).

Four weeks is, indeed, a rather short time to rehearse and the actors' complaints may appear to have validity. But actors always want more time. Saint-Denis rehearsed his 1961 production of *The Cherry Orchard* for twelve weeks and the same complaints were heard. American and British actors often speak with envy of the extraordinarily long rehearsal time that the Moscow Arts Theatre has at its disposal: months and months to develop a character. Yet, when complimented on the excellence of his *Cherry Orchard*, a leading member of the Arts Theater replied with great seriousness, "No. It could have been much better. We only rehearsed for eight months, and it shows it."

During run-throughs, the director's relationship to the cast has again changed. His distance is now established and he has become the surrogate audience and drama critic. The director's primary contact with the actor is through note sessions and brush-up rehearsals. The stage manager has now taken charge, beginning the gradual process of breaking the cast in to a performance routine. For the first time, the actors hear instructions that will be repeated during performance: "Five minutes, please." "Ok. Places!" "Curtain!" "Fifteen minute break. Please don't be late. I want to get the second act up on time." Questions that the actor previously asked the director are now deflected to the stage manager. Such questions, often from very experienced actors whom one would think should know better, reflect the tenacity, the adhesiveness of the bond between the actor and director. They are subtle ways in which some actors try to relate to the director as if it were still the earlier phase of rehearsals.

The actor's need for the director can also be seen by the way in which he awaits the director's comments. Some sit quietly, but expectantly; others will read a newspaper, glancing up only when they are referred to, in an attempt to deny their dependency; still others sit studiously with pads and pencils, prepared to take down notes from their teacher. It is not uncommon to see a line of actors waiting to speak to the director privately after the entire company has been dismissed.

Ideally, an actor tries to respond to most of the notes he receives creatively, not mechanically. Although the director's comments are now stated in result terms ("Do it faster." "Speak more softly to her."), the actor attempts to translate these instructions into process terms, just as he originally did with the author's instructions, given to him by the text in the form of dialogue and stage directions. He must justify the instruction by finding something within the reality of the scene which will result in giving the director what he wants. For instance, "Speak more softly to her" may be accomplished by the actor's intensification of his belief that there are other people in the next room who might overhear what he is saying. Once this aspect of the situation is remembered and reactivated, the actor will find that he does not have to make himself "speak more softly." His character quite naturally and spontaneously lowers his voice at the right moment. In such ways, the actor has avoided artificiality; he has also reinforced his own sense of truth.

In addition to note sessions, the director may choose to re-rehearse certain scenes. He must decide whether a scene has to be taken apart again, reanalyzed, rebuilt from the ground up. In this case, such a scene may not have much consistency and strength during the next few run-throughs. Does the director want to take a chance that the scene will improve on its own? Or must he commit the cast to a regression in the work, throwing the next few run-throughs out of balance, chancing, in this case, some demoralization and increased anxiety? Such a regression is hard to stop; it may result in other scenes falling apart on their own. As we will see, taking a scene apart again actually gratifies the actor's deep wish to return to the honeymoon of the opening phase.

If, on the other hand, run-throughs are progressing smoothly, if the actors and director sense a deepening of the work, then the director can use his limited rehearsal time in more creative ways. Improvisations, for instance, can be extremely useful even at this stage because they strengthen the actor's belief in the play and reinforce his feeling that he understands the character, that he and the character are one. In such an exercise, an "imaginary" situation, one not in the text, is presented to the actor-characters; they are asked to improvise dialogue and movements as if this were part of the reality of the play.

Directors have also found it useful to ask actors to speak aloud the thoughts of their characters at the same time as the text of the play is being spoken aloud. (Brecht is credited with inventing this exercise.) One director invariably has his cast lie down on comfortable mats in a pitch black room and speak through the entire play, while picturing all their accompanying physical activity. This brings the actor close to the sleep-state where there is a reduction in outside stimuli and access to motor activity is drastically limited. In such a situation, the actor's imagination is highly stimulated, almost as if he were dreaming the play. His inner world of the play becomes overinvested with psychic energy because this energy does not have access to paths of motor discharge as in waking life. Another director will have the cast do a complete run-through of the play with no one watching them, not even the director himself or the stage management staff.

The purpose of such work is twofold: first, to strengthen the actors' sense of truth; and second, to give them the confidence that the play has become their own.

This run-through stage is the last major opportunity that the director has to make sure the acting values of his production have achieved excellence. The cast is about to enter the arduous, frustrating, distracting period of technical rehearsals where the emphasis shifts to the physical aspects of the production. Because run-throughs offer the final opportunity to "get it right," directors will resort to any tactic to accomplish this end. The niceties of theory and technique, outlined above, can be jettisoned. What we might call "emergency measures" are in order. What makes such tactics definable as "emergency" is their timing: directors talk in result terms all the time; specific how-to-do-it instructions are given even during the first week of rehearsals.

Taking an entire scene apart again—fragmenting it, reexamining the basic objectives—is an example of an emer-

gency measure. Others can be easily illustrated. The director now tells an actor what to do and shows him how to do
it. Many actors have experienced this "tell and show" as a
mini-defeat, a narcissistic blow, because it implies that the
actor did not have the resources (creativity) to solve the
problem himself. They usually experience such an intervention as limiting their autonomy. To some extent it has; it is
an externally imposed prohibition or injunction, which the
actor hears as "Thou shalt do it my way." In addition,
directors may find it essential to have a private conference
with an actor in which he talks solely in result terms, that is,
from the spectator-critic point of view. He may now have to
say, for example, "Look! She is a cruel, sadistic, ambitious
woman and, quite frankly, I'm not getting that." One can
imagine how devastating this comment could be for the
actress playing Goneril, especially with only six days left
before opening.

It was during this phase of the work that an "emergency
measure" was used with the actors who were doing the
prison play. The homosexuality, paranoia, and jealousy
had been effectively established quite early in the work. But
the visceral sense that these men were actually in jail, the
underlying claustrophobia was not there. Most of the actors
came from upper-middle-class families; the closest they had
ever come to jail was traffic court.

After the second run-through, the director proposed a
visit to the city jail; arrangements had been made with the
police department to let the actors "explore" a cell. Appearing a bit ill at ease, the principals entered the cell, saw the
beds, the toilet bowl, the dirty sink; they began to get the
feel of the "place." At that point, the director locked the cell
door to intensify their experience. Again, they readily con-
sented. Once the door was locked, the guard and the director left. Actors E, F, and H remained imprisoned for several
hours. Actor E later described the initial fury they all felt
toward the director: their sense of disbelief and disorientation ("Could he really be serious about this?"); their
threats to call their agents, their lawyers, their union (none
of them thought of calling their families); their renewed
pleas for release to the police guards.

The run-through the next day was an immense success,

as was the opening night. But the happy ending is not the purpose of this lengthy illustration. By resorting to such a drastic emergency measure, the director had given the cast several clear messages: something was wrong with the acting and he was using his power as director to fix it. Needless to say, the relationship between the actors and the director had irrevocably changed, not only during the final days of work on this play, but on all subsequent productions in which they collaborated. Actor F asked, "How can you ever trust a guy like that again?" I shall return to this incident later. Because many of the actors experienced an unusually high degree of stage fright, an examination of this production's dynamics will give us valuable insight into the intrapsychic state of affairs of the actors on opening night.

Technical rehearsals add all the physical elements to the production: sets, costumes, props, furniture, makeup, lights, sound effects, and music. During techs and dresses, actors work a twelve-hour day for one week. The director and his cast have the experience of being locked up in the place (the theater) where the opening will inevitably happen. The entirety of the actor's waking life is devoted to this final push toward public performance. (The actor's dream-life is also working over the production, but I will defer dealing with this issue until we come to consider the stage fright attack itself.) Outside stimuli are reduced; concerns about the actor's real family, for example, are superseded by those about his cast-family. Some actors begin to decorate their dressing rooms to make them "feel more at home." During techs and dresses, actors also like to sit out in "the house" to watch the mise-en-scène develop. This gives them a kind of security; they will be supported by excellent visual elements. But it is frequently difficult to get certain cast members to remain backstage during the final dresses. Some will say they do not like the feeling of being "cooped up." Others seem to be identifying with the director: they make comments about the visual elements in the same way he does.

It is impossible to describe systematically the events of this final stage: the elations and depressions, the governing pressure of the clock-calendar, the fatigue, the craving for stimulants. This is a far cry from the relaxed flexibility of the opening phase. Accidents plague the process; unpredictability increases the pressure. One light cue can take forty-five minutes to resolve. A quick costume change can stop the whole procedure for half an hour, only to be shelved until the entire costume is rebuilt in the shop. Doors on the set don't stay shut; the curtain inexplicably falls during the middle of the act; the deafening sound of "a cock crowing" is suddenly heard in the middle of "O, what a rogue and peasant slave am I."

Clearly, the director-actor relationship has undergone yet another radical change. The onset of run-throughs tended to distance the director from his cast; the stage manager began to take over certain of his functions. But now the director is not primarily concerned about the actors at all; his attention seems focused entirely on the physical elements. "At least during run-throughs he was watching our work. Now he's spending more goddamn time with that fucking, incompetent excuse for a lighting designer. He should fire the prick. Christ!" The fact that Actor K could verbalize his anger is, from the production's point of view, a prognostically good sign. By becoming a spokesman, so to speak, for the entire company's anger at being deserted, he clears the air and with luck prevents such anger from turning inward onto the self. Unfortunately, this was only temporary. At the final dress rehearsal, Actor K accidentally fell off the stage and broke his leg.

At the start of technicals, Director M used to say to his cast, "I'm sorry to tell you that I have to go away for a few days; I have to leave you in the capable hands of our stage manager." Most actors reacted with surprise, some with dismay and shock. When the director qualified this by explaining that he only meant a figurative departure—a shift of attention from them to the technical elements—the sighs of relief, coupled with nervous laughter and frequent expressions of disgust at his "joke," attested to the depth of the actor-director bond. The disgust and nervous laughter represented some actors' resentment at having been caught out, having been forced to acknowledge that such a strong attachment exists. Vomiting, on open night, is a frequent manifestation of stage fright. Disgust also figures in the actor's relation to the audience, where feeding fantasies are more overt (see chap. 4).[11]

The essence of the final dress rehearsal is that it be an exact replica of what will happen on opening night without, of course, the presence of an audience. A small group of friends is invited to give the company a feel for potential responses as well as a sense of the "pitch of the house." This final dress rehearsal echoes the first run-through (approximately ten days before), which also followed a period of interruptions and distractions.

There are no athletic cheers at the end of the evening. The leading players exchange few words with each other. They are already retreating into a solitude, a protective shield which must carry them through the next twenty-four hours. The evening often ends in silence. While young, naive beginners tend to be buoyed up with the confidence of a successful dress, the older, more experienced professionals know how unpredictable an opening night can be. Somewhat stoically, these pros leave it all in the hands of fate. "It's just one gigantic crap shoot" is the way Actor S put it.

The director briefly addresses the company at the end of the evening. Even though he will see the actors tomorrow, he will never again relate to them in the same way. The actors now know that the complete responsibility for the success or failure of the enterprise is theirs. The director, having started out as an ally, companion, collaborator, must be given up. Now he belongs to a different world: somehow he is *out there*, not *in here*.

Child's Play

We can now afford to take a moment's rest in our narrative of the actor's movement from the privacy of his own work on himself toward the encounter with the audience. The dress rehearsal is over and the actor is in the process of transformation from the rehearsing-actor to the performing-actor. While he is, figuratively speaking, asleep, we can continue our work and take stock of where we have gotten so far, reviewing the acting and rehearsal process from a more explicitly psychoanalytic point of view.

As we have seen, the actor comes to depend upon the director in a particular way. This dependency is an outgrowth of the nature of the acting process. Certain basic ego functions essential to the preparation of a role, such as memory, perception, self-observation, and self-evaluation, are temporarily blocked. Caught in this predicament, the actor resolves it by permitting the director to perform some of these functions for him. Throughout their work together, the director acts as a partial auxiliary ego for the actor.

This dependency sets the stage for the activation of "transference reactions" during the rehearsal process, reactions which are only finally resolved during performance. The notion of transference is usually associated with the (psychoanalytic) therapeutic session but the phenomenon can exist outside of the patient-doctor relationship. In fact, Freud once noted that "the less its presence is suspected, the more powerfully it operates" (1910 [1909], p. 51). As for a working definition, we can do no better than the following: "The displacement of patterns of feelings and behavior, originally experienced with significant figures of one's childhood, to individuals in one's current relationships. This unconscious process thus brings about a repetition, not consciously perceived, of attitudes, fantasies and emotions of love, hate, anger, etc. under many different circumstances" (Moore and Fine, 1968, p. 92.)[12]

The director is experienced by the actor in many different, often conflicting, ways: as boss, tyrant, companion, collaborator, critic, confidant, teacher. In these guises, the director nurtures the actor's performance; he helps it grow. He protects the actor from disturbing outside stimuli by controlling the working environment. Through rehearsals, he can, among other things encourage, advise, gently criticize, scold, implore, cajole, ridicule, and command the actor.

Actors commonly refer to themselves as "children" or involved in childish things and describe their director as "father," "father-confessor," and the like. Such remarks are rarely made seriously but beneath their surface humor or sarcasm, we can discern the grain of an unconscious truth. For example, Laurence Olivier once remarked, "It does seem sometimes that acting is hardly the occupation for an adult. False noses, lots of make-up and gum on my face" (Cottrell 1975, p. 357). Mike Nichols said that acting "brings out a person's childishness, the baby portion. Directing encourages the more adult portion of your character—the father part" (Gelb 1977, p. 40). And Little and Cantor (1970) quote Maureen Stapleton: "We are the dock rats, the deformed children of the world" (p. 114; Stapleton experiences severe stage fright; see p. 62).

"Father-confessor," as we have seen, also rings true. The intimacies shared with the director are often secrets that have never been divulged to any other person, for example, Actor G's intense loneliness. Many directors see themselves as a father or as a counselor to a group of children. Alan Schneider even included the playwright, whom he perceived as "his wife." For Schneider, then, it is truly a "family," which works on and presents the play to the public (Little and Cantor 1970, pp. 153–54). Quite early in his career, Elia Kazan received the nickname Gadge. This stands for "gadget," the one who could fix anything. When *Cat on a Hot Tin Roof* opened, I found that actors had dubbed me "Big Daddy" after one of the central characters in the play. This nickname is a fine example of the ambivalence that actors feel toward directors: in *Cat*, Big Daddy is dying of cancer.

Some actors are extremely possessive of their director, referring to him as "*my* director," often with a noticeable childlike affective coloration to the possessive pronoun. They want him to show them what to do and how to do it but directors do not like to work with actors who have to be "spoon-fed," to use the infantalizing colloquialism for actors who have very little initiative. This excessive need to imitate reflects one way in which the actor-director relationship mirrors the child-parent one.[13] Actors want "a mommy" or "a daddy" to show them what to do and, in very difficult scenes, ones in which frightening, unconscious fantasies are aroused, the "Show me what to do" can even become "Do it for me!"

Marian Seldes (1978) describes in detail the relationship between Tallulah Bankhead and Tony Richardson (pp. 210–15). During rehearsals, they were clearly at odds with each other. Their working styles clashed. Here are two verbatim transcripts from rehearsals.

TALLULAH: How shall I read this, darling?
TONY: I prefer to hear what you feel, darling.
TALLULAH: You're a great help.

TALLULAH: How shall I say this?
TONY: Any way you want.
TALLULAH: You're the director.
TONY: Well, *invent*. You are the actress.
TALLULAH: I signed the wrong contract. I'm sending you back to Oxford.

Bankhead was asking for help in the form of "show me how to do it"; the director was frustrating her need. In retaliation, she made Richardson into the child, sending him back to school. Publicly, Bankhead insulted Richardson; privately, she missed him. When he flew to London for a brief weekend holiday, she was "furious" at him; she felt "he deserted us." The inappropriateness and ambivalence of her behavior is firmly established by the fact that Bankhead would never praise Richardson to his face: only, and often, behind his back.[14]

At the same time, the director can be perceived as, and of course often is, a threatening figure. There are many directors who actually provoke aggression in order "to get a performance out of an actor." The actors' anticipatory fear of the director is revealed by their surprise at "how nice he was to work with" or how easily "he made me feel at home." But images of the nurturing, helpful parent coexist with those of the stern, prohibiting, hurtful one. Jailing the actors for serveral hours contributed to a regressive reactivation of the image of an all-powerful father-director. Offering the following direction, "Watch those Jewish hands, Seldes," turned the director into a fearful, sadistic figure (Seldes 1978, p. 138). Interestingly enough, actors have a need to regain contact with an image of the idealized parent-director; Marian Seldes came to appreciate the "good" in John Dexter (1978, pp. 140–43; for Geraldine Page's somewhat similar response to this same director, see p. 126).

Some actors will deny their need for the director's attention and help. They will criticize him mercilessly but do so in such a way as to suggest that these angry feelings function to ward off tender, loving ones. When they are alone with each other, perhaps at lunch or in the green room during a break, he is usually a constant topic of conversation (see Seldes 1978, pp. 206 ff.). Furthermore, the "star," who must control the casting conference, is often avoiding dependency needs. Wanting to advise the director on other casting decisions, on the choice of set and costume designers, and even on the interpretation of the play is a way of furthering this denial by taking over the director's functions, by obliterating him. The obliteration takes place almost consciously; at an unconscious level, by assuming the director's role, this "star" is identifying with him and preserving an intrapsychic relationship. Actress C has stated publicly that the best directors she has had are the ones who stayed out of her way; she protests that she is the kind of actress who needs virtually no direction at all. Yet, when rehearsing a new play in London, she frequently called a colleague in New York, asking for advice on how to play the part.

The actor works within what we might call "a regressive context." In effect, the director says to the child within the actor, "Come play in front of me and I'll make sure you don't get seriously hurt." The director promotes a freedom of association-in-play. The actor's training has prepared him to accept just such an offer: a license to regress, to bring to bear the full play of his unconscious on the scene.[15]

One of the hallmarks of the objective, the "I want," is that it be conceived of in the positive, never the negative. "I don't want him to leave" is useless because it does not suggest or compel action. When recast in the positive, however, "I want to force him to stay," the actor finds he has numerous options open to him, all of which will result in activity. Furthermore, the actor's license to try anything, that is, to act on any impulse, is another cornerstone of the

rehearsal-game. Similarly, two major aspects of unconscious mental life are that the concept "no" does not exist
and instinctual drives, in the form of wishes, are continually
pressing for gratification, that is to say, for immediate discharge. Therefore, the actor's work inevitably brings him
closer to his own unconscious: "no" cannot exist in an
actable objective and "try anything" allows for immediate
discharge of instinctual tensions.

Take this as an example. During the opening phase of
work, Actor J had chosen as his objective, "I want to escape
from them." In accomplishing this, he knocked down two
burly actors, overturned a card table, threw a chair across
the room, and ended up by breaking another actor's arm.
Although this is *not* acting, but "acting out," it does illustrate the regressive aspect of the work: there is only "yes"
and the impulse has to be gratified at once. Unlike dreaming, where the ego's access to motility is reduced because of
the sleep-state, Actor J's ego still retained, rather unfortunately for his partners, its ability to generate physical
activity.

This example, I hasten to add, might be classified as the
psychopathology of everyday acting. Once a regressive
movement has been instituted, it may be difficult to control
its extent or depth. Actor J's judgment and reality-testing
were temporarily impaired and his director was not fulfilling his part of the bargain. Recognizing the early warning
signs of this explosion, the director might have stepped in
as a surrogate for Actor J's compromised ego-functioning.
But the director served neither as an auxiliary ego nor superego. In fact, the director's own aggressive impulses in-
terfered with his ego functioning in the sense that their
vicarious gratification became more important to him than
his actor's safety.[16] Finally, since J's chosen objective in the
scene, "to escape from them," was repeated later in his life
as a need "to escape from C" (his director), it is possible to
speculate that J's inappropriate behavior indicated an unconscious fear of his strong bond with C. His excessive
violence in the scene was an "acting out" of the transference
wish to escape from his dependency. Up to this point in his
life, Actor J had done his best work with C. Colleagues and
drama critics were beginning to wonder whether J was truly

gifted or whether it was the director's gift in knowing "just what strings to pull."

The director's job, of course, is to rehearse the play and, using whatever means are at his disposal, to get the best performance possible from the actor. Directors are aware in some way that they appeal to the "baby portion" within the actor but, in general, they remain unaware of the deep psychic significance of their link to the child within the man. In view of the regressive context, then, the director temporarily takes over certain defensive functions for the actor to protect him from a more severe regression, the kind of regression we have witnessed in the previous example. Although most directors are certainly not aware of it, their control of the rehearsal has the effect of diminishing the actor's unconscious anxiety about the regressive context of the work. Because the actor's observing ego is temporarily compromised, while his participating ego—the performing self—fully engages in the rehearsal-game, the director performs an observing function that goes far beyond giving criticism of the work. This observing function—a reliable mirror—helps to keep the actor in touch with himself by reinforcing the actor's capacity to separate fantasy from reality. (This issue will be dealt with more extensively in chap. 5.)

In the early- and middle-phase rehearsals, the director is always there. This in itself is reassuring to the actor. Furthermore, delaying work on an intensely emotional scene gives the actor more time to personalize basic aspects of the character's objectives and, at the same time, serves a protective, anxiety-controlling function. It seems to me that many directors have erred by forcing an actor too quickly into areas of a role that he was not yet capable of handling. Too much unconscious anxiety was mobilized and the performance failed, in part, because the actor had been frightened away from his character.

We have already come across other methods of controlling the regression and its resultant anxiety: the order in which an actor is introduced to his character, the time allotted to each scene, and, of course, the intensity and depth of interpretations. By far the simplest is to interrupt a scene with a straightforward "Good. We've gone far enough with that today. Let's sleep on it." Nevertheless, things do heat up during an intense rehearsal. Actor G's Hamlet was clearly moving too quickly toward a physically violent resolution of his confrontation with Ophelia. The director stopped the scene and delivered a short talk on the meaning of the word, "nunnery," in Elizabethan England and linked it to the way in which the scene begins, "Nymph, in thy orisons/Be all my sins remembered" (III.i.89). While it was not the director's intention to do so, what, in fact, he had initiated was an intellectualizing defense for the actor, a shift in accent from the emotional to the cognitive sphere.

But such interactions can be of a more primitive sort. Abruptly stopping a scene when Willy Loman was about to hit Biff, the director had to take the actor-Willy off the set, a firm arm around his shoulder. The actor's body was rigid; the director's embrace let him know that the rage could be contained just as the director's presence reminded the actor that, after all, this was only a game. The director had become a stimulus barrier, a protective shield for the actor's ego, which was in danger of being temporarily overwhelmed by too much aggressive energy.

These examples, by the way, indicate yet another reason for the actor's tendency to idealize the director, namely, an unconscious awareness of the need for an objective and reliable referee. The actor senses that the director is the keeper of the ego's integrating or synthesizing function. A typical exchange between actors, revealing both the fear and the reassurance, is: "I'm all mixed up about this part. Does he really know what he's doing?" "Don't worry. I've worked with him before. He's got it all in his head."

On the other hand, one can sometimes infer that actors are unconsciously instituting certain mechanisms of defense to protect themselves against a deeper regression. Actor E, rehearsing the closet scene in *Hamlet*, manifested intense, inappropriate rage toward the Ghost, who interrupts Hamlet's confrontation with his mother (III.iv). In early rehearsals, "My father, in his habit as he lived," was said with great venom. The rage was appropriate in response to Gertrude but the actor could not yet bring himself to deal with his own feelings about "mother" and so could not fulfill the demands of the scene. Isolation of affect, to use the psychoanalytic term for this type of defense, was the result. The ideational content of the mother-son scene was portrayed in all its textual, verbal clarity, and yet it was devoid of any feeling. The affect had been displaced onto the interrupting father where it made no sense.[17]

A final, rather charming example, illustrates a self-generated defense mechanism. Mike Nichols, directing *The Graduate*, interpreted Mrs. Robinson's "low opinion of her-self" to Anne Bancroft. Nichols's description continues: "She said, 'Oh, that's terrific! Oh, yes, thank you, I under-stand, that's absolutely wonderful.' When we got to that scene, i.e., to rehearse it, I asked, 'What happened to that thing I told you?' She said, 'Oh, I forgot, I forgot'" (Probst 1975, p. 117). This forgetting is a relatively common exam-ple of repression at work. It is not uncommon for actors to respond, as Bancroft did, with such effusive gratitude to-ward the director, but one must be a bit wary of such overreactions. Sometimes, they signal that an interpreta-tion has resonated too deeply within the actor, resulting in a "forgetting."

The director's interaction with the actor is not dissimilar to Winnicott's notions of "good-enough mothering" (1960*a*, p. 145) and "the holding environment" (1960*b*, p. 47). The director attempts to create a "facilitating environment" in early rehearsals. While continuing to look at the bond that ties the actor to his director, we can also gain a deeper understanding of those imaginative, intrapsychic processes involved in building a character.

One of the central myths or metaphors of theater is that of "the child" as "the role to be born" (Stanislavski 1936, p. 295). This is one of the ways in which actors think (pre-consciously) about their work and, as with all myths, a psychological truth is being expressed. Stanislavski (1936) said, "Our type of creativeness is the conception and birth of a new being—the person in the part. It is a natural act similar to the birth of a human being" (p. 294). And a bit later on, "The period of gestation for a part is at least as long as that of a human being, and often considerably longer. If you analyse this process you will be convinced that laws regulate organic nature, whether she is creating a new phenomenon biologically or imaginatively" (p. 295). One wonders how the member of the Moscow Arts Theatre, who apologized for the shortness of rehearsal time—eight months—would have felt had the baby been full term.

Stanislavski refers to "the birth of a human being" but I am inclined to see the maturation of a character as being akin to the birth of the ego and "the psychological birth of the human infant" (Mahler, Pine, and Bergmann 1975). This psychoanalytic perspective of ego development sheds light on yet another way in which the actor experiences the director: as "mother" to both the actor and the character.

In what follows, I will talk about the director speaking to the character. This avoids the rather cumbersome locution of phrases like "the character developing within the actor" or the actor as he begins to live "into the role," the latter being the way Stanislavski put it (1936, p. 295). But this is exactly what does happen in rehearsals, namely, the director refers to the actor by the character's name. I have even seen some directors relate to the actor as if he already possessed some of the personality traits of the character. There is always an ambiguity here: to whom is the director talking? Actress B or Blanche? Actually, psychotherapists work with such ambiguities daily and understand their implications better than stage directors. Therapists are speaking simultaneously to the adult male in the consultation room and to the child-within-the-man in the patient's unconscious.

Coincident with the earliest phases of life, a set of functions, pertaining to adaptation with the environment, begin to develop into a structure that we label "ego." This is, in part, a response to frustrations from the environment. As ego tries to mediate between the demands of instinctual wishes pressing for gratification and the necessities imposed upon it by the external world, "good-enough mothering" is able to modulate the stress from the environment, maintaining at a tolerable level the amount of frustration necessary for growth. By her empathic, encouraging, nurturing responses to the infant, the mother functions as an auxiliary ego for him and as a reliable mirror. The director's role is similar.

Building a character begins with a choice of objectives,

the "I want." In this way, the inner needs of the character are defined and explored. At a primitive level, the "I want" represents a hunger for something; it is, in fact, the representation of a wish. Early rehearsals, based as they are on answering the question How am I going to get it? have to do with attempts at fulfilling a wish. Furthermore, since a wish is a derivative of an unconscious instinctual impulse, there is, I believe, a helpful analogy to be made between the actor's "I want" and an instinctual impulse as Freud defined it in 1915. An instinct has a source, an aim and an object; so does the actor's "I want." While the source of the actor's objective cannot be easily located, its aim and its object are well defined: "I want to do something [the aim] to someone [the object]."[18]

In this sense, the birth of a character begins within a matrix of instinctual impulses (objectives) pressing toward discharge. But the acting out of these objectives leads to an interaction with the play's environment: the other characters' needs, the given circumstances, the present situation, and so forth. Inevitably, the environment puts obstacles in the character's path: wishes cannot be so easily fulfilled, conflicts develop, the character must adapt his behavior in order to achieve gratification. In other words, if the objective is analogous to the instinctual impulse, then the ways in which the actor tries to fulfill his objective are analogous to the progressive differentiation of ego functions.

The director helps the character stand up for his rights, gratify his needs, deal with the anger and frustration that accrues from environmental opposition or indifference at a time when the character is still, metaphorically speaking, in his infancy. The director tries to do no more but no less than the character seems to need at a particular moment in his development. (Characters, like infants, can be babied too much.) Here is an example of how a director gently lets the character-child know that accommodation to the outside world is a fact of life. It comes from a rehearsal of Arthur Miller's *After the Fall*. "On the second or third day . . . [Frank] Langella started talking about the 'plight' of Quentin. The actresses who play Quentin's wives and lovers, among them Miss Wiest, shouted him down. Mr. Langella, worried, asked Mr. Tillinger [the director], 'What are we going to do?' The director replied, 'They're playing their parts'" (Freedman 1984). But as rehearsals proceed, the character begins to succeed on his own; he see what works and what does not. His skill at adaptation improves. The character's ego functions mature within the facilitating environment of the rehearsal.[19]

Thus, the director functions as an auxiliary ego both for the actor and the character. For the actor, the director mainly takes over certain primary, autonomous functions of the ego; for the character, the director performs those adaptive functions, relating to conflict with the environment, without which the character might never develop at all. For both actor and character, the director serves as a stimulus barrier. The actor in turn experiences the director's nurturing in a global fashion because he, the actor, does not want to distinguish between himself and the character. The protection he receives from the director, whether it be to preserve his own autonomy as creator, or the autonomy of that which he has created, amounts to the same thing. (This is the director in his transference role as "mother"; see pp. 127–28.)

Furthermore, equating the actor's "I want" with a wish, an instinctual impulse, clarifies the mechanism of personalization, the way the actor makes total use of himself. By concentrating on the "I want," the actor inevitably invests his own unconscious wishes with emotional significance. This additional "sum of excitation" infuses the actor's performance with vitality and authenticity. Invariably, such wishes are embedded within memories; hence, Stanislavski's emphasis on emotion memory exercises. In short, the "I want" links up with a repressed wish which makes available to the actor the appropriate affective coloration for the scene.

The changes in the actor-director relationship during the middle and final rehearsal phases adumbrate the events of opening night. The distancing between the actor and director, hinted at in the middle phase and actualized in the final phase, along with the pressures accompanying the actor's deeper personalization of the role, force the actor to adjust to the director's new position. He has been keenly aware of the director's physical closeness: his eyes, voice, touch, and smell. Now he must cope with the loss of this type of contact. The emphasis shifts to the director's entire body: perceived, at first, ten to fifteen feet away behind a desk, later, as a dimly lit figure at the stage manager's control console in the auditorium. If early rehearsals represent a "oneness" with the director, then later phases imply a "separateness." (I shall return to this issue in chap. 5, where several extended passages from Louise Kaplan's book *Oneness and Separateness* are introduced to highlight the similarities between the actor-director and the child-mother dyad.)

A distinction between the rehearsing- and the performing-actor will be made shortly. But a similar distinction can also be made between the opening-phase and the final-phase director to indicate two things: (1) the different functions that the director performs for the actor in each of these phases; and (2) the different fantasies within the actor that accrue to the director's changing functions. It is the opening-phase director that the actor does not want to lose. This figure is associated with the most pleasurable stages of the work during which the actor-character begins "a love affair with the world." The opening-phase director has become the object of and helped revive pleasurable memories from the actor's own childhood when he could joyfully and fearlessly play in front of mother. The need to keep this director alive is very strong indeed.[20]

The actor unconsciously resists separateness by whatever means he has at his disposal: the late night telephone calls, the inappropriate behavior generated by the shift of focus onto the stage manager, the complaints about too little rehearsal time, the resentment when the director turns his attention to technical details during the dress rehearsals—all these actions represent the wish to go back to the honeymoon of the earlier phase. Similarly, taking apart a scene during the final phase (an emergency measure) is very risky because the final-phase director engages the actors in what might be called phase-inappropriate behavior. Appearing to them once again as the opening-phase director, he stimulates nurturing fantasies that contain the fear of the loss of the facilitating environment which he, the director, has fostered.

Such a state of affairs intensifies the actor's conflict between the progressive movement toward autonomous performance and the regressive pull of the pleasures of early work. The deterioration of other scenes signifies the actor's way of coping with the conflict: he gives up on the scene, unconsciously wishing to be taken care of again. He also expresses anger toward the abandonment by the opening-phase director; in effect he is saying "See what a bad director you are. You really couldn't help me." Moreover, an "I'll leave him before he leaves me" phenomenon is also quite common. Actors start "performing" the play in the middle phase and maintain that they can't wait until the opening night has arrived. Paradoxically, such actors will often be the same ones who are complaining about the lack of rehearsal time.

Difficulty in learning lines can often signify a resistance to separation. The actual script of the play has become the concrete representation of the *part* the actor has been given or has wrested from the director. But it is also associated with the pleasures of the closeness to the opening-phase director. Actress A, for example, will not permit anyone to look at her script during rehearsals. She claims that she writes down very personal notes to herself. When, without thinking, a director started to look at her script, she reacted with defensive anger. Apparently, she writes down almost everything the director says; she was embarrassed at his seeing how much she "hung on his every word."

Giving up the script has other ramifications as well: it forces the actor to face the fact that someday he will have to give up the opening-phase director; it also implies that the actor is expected to work in a more autonomous way. Because the script is the first concrete support from the environment that the actor "incorporates," its internalization carries the meaning "I can now take care of these lines of dialogue myself." The script may also function as a "transitional object" for the actor-character; it permits him to carry the director-part around with him as he is testing out the reality of the play's environment. In this sense, giving up the script is very much like giving up the mothering aspect of the director who functions as a bridge for the actor between "in here" and "out there" (Winnicott 1951).

The fear of losing the director's function as an observing ego can promote a maladaptive, defensive global identification with him. Actors start "playing director": they criticize each other's work, reinterpret the meaning of the play, and evaluate the mise-en-scène. Sometimes the anger at the final-phase director is focused on his lost, or being lost "presence" in the actor's mind; such a mechanism was at work in Actor K, who broke his leg on the night of the dress rehearsal.[21]

There is, however, an adaptive way in which the actor can maintain this relationship, namely, by selectively identifying with certain functions that the director performed for him. This is all to the good. Because the actor knows that he alone will be performing the play, he must begin to develop the capacity to observe his own work. In early rehearsals the director's interventions were primarily aimed at the actor's participating ego, not at his observing ego. In fact, the director intentionally fostered this particular type of division in the mind. He reinforced the emergence of the participating ego (the character) at the expense of its observing, reflecting counterpart. Now the actor must begin a process of reinternalization of his own self-observing functions without, of course, becoming self-conscious in a maladaptive way.[22] This is the essence of the transformation from the rehearsing-actor to the performing-actor.

Under optimal circumstances the difficulties of the final rehearsal phase are overcome. It seems possible that many performances fail in part because the intrapsychic conflicts I have been describing are not recognized or effectively dealt with. Of primary importance in this regard is that a strong working alliance between actor and director has been established from the start. This reality-oriented aspect of the relationship helps both parties weather the storm of the final phase. While most directors are not aware of the implications of (unconscious) transference reactions, all of them are certainly clear about the necessity of establishing good rapport with their actors. This factor affects the casting of a play: can we work together? It is uppermost in the director's mind as he begins to rehearse. Supportive interventions, based upon a realistic assessment of an actor's achievement in a scene, continually reinforce the roots of this working alliance. Most actors, regardless of their experience, can develop suspicious, paranoidlike traits toward the director in the final phase. They are touchy about too many notes—"He doesn't like it"—or about too few notes—"He's given up on me." Directors are usually prepared for such ambivalence.

In the final phase, then, the actor is doing the play for the director and, of course, at the deepest level for himself. "I want to get help from him" has now been replaced by "I want to give him what he wants." The actor senses that he can produce something worthwhile, something which will elicit approval from the final-phase director. "Will he be there to feed me so that I can grow into the character?" represents the primitive and primary anxiety at separation from the opening-phase director. The conflict in this early phase is between trust and mistrust. "Will he love me for what I've produced?" represents anxiety at the loss of being loved by the final-phase director. Here, the conflict is between initiative-autonomy and shame-doubt (Erikson 1950).[23] During performance, the actor's unconscious wish to be fed is going to be transferred onto the audience. "Will he love me for what I've produced?" is transformed into the plural. It is, perhaps, the most obvious aspect of the actor-audience relationship as "they" now take their seats.

The Performing-Actor

The final dress rehearsal is an exact replica of the opening night, except for the audience. With its arrival, the rehearsal suddenly becomes a performance and the rehearsing-actor becomes a performing-actor, someone who has to develop the capacity to be, at one and the same time, inside the character and outside him. The rehearsing-actor submits himself to his performing ego, censoring almost nothing, depending upon the director to fulfill the observer role. Later in the work, the actor internalizes some of the director's functions and so is able to benefit from this adaptive split in the ego. He has learned how to maintain a self-observing ego without diminishing the activity and spontaneity of its participating counterpart, that is, the performing ego.

Otis Skinner, for example, observed that "I have never known a great actor to 'lose himself in his part' (as the saying goes); he may be in a state of great exultation but unless he has completely lost his self control he can never forget that he is on a stage, before an audience, and has a part to play" (1938, p. 280). Florence Eldridge went so far as to call performing "a schizophrenic experience. You're working on two levels. You try to recapture fantasy each night. And then the editorial part of your mind begins to function, coolly monitoring the fantasy part of you, making intellectual comments on your performance" (Little and Cantor 1970, p. 120).

Some examples, the first two from performances, the third from a final dress rehearsal, illustrate what Skinner and Eldridge are talking about. Near the end of the second act of *The Importance of Being Earnest*, John Gielgud was working so well that he actually was getting too many laughs. In comedy, a given scene can only support so much laughter. A laugh is an interruption of the action, and if too many come in quick succession, they can blow the fabric of the scene apart. The actors then have a very difficult time in drawing the audience back into the action of the play. During laughter, the audience's attention shifts from the actors onto itself; too many laughs ultimately interfere with the audience's "willing suspension of disbelief."

As Gielgud approached the climax of the scene, which included a major laugh line he was unwilling to give up, he conveniently sipped some tea precisely at the moment before he was to deliver his punch line. And, before speaking the line, he brought his tea cup sharply down onto its saucer, creating a loud click in the theater, silencing the entire audience. In the setting of the hush he had created, Gielgud rather quietly delivered his line. There was an explosion of laughter. To the audience, Gielgud remained in character, and the scene maintained its forward movement. There was no interruption of the illusion of the play. Gielgud was functioning on two levels at the same time.

The actor who was appearing as Kent to Gielgud's Lear

was late for his entrance into the storm scene. Kent's actual line is "Who's there?" but the actor, rattled by his lateness, blurted out, "Are you there?" Gielgud, having just finished one of Lear's most difficult speeches ("Blow winds, and crack your cheeks; Rage! Blow!"), replied *sotto voce*, "Yes, Germantown 3824," his own home telephone number.

At a dress rehearsal, after he had spoken his first fifteen lines as Hamlet, Actor B stopped the scene. (Fifteen lines of iambic pentameter run just under one minute.) He looked to the director in the balcony, saying, "Excuse me, G, I have to stop. I seem to have lost the pitch of the house. Can you help me find it?"

Actor B had performed in this theater thousands of times before; he knew its "pitch." Given the acoustical properties of the hall, Actor B knew the reverberation time of his own voice at a specific volume. Because he planned to whisper large portions of a later soliloquy, it was essential that the audience hear every word. (Approximately two hours later: "Now might I do it pat, now he is praying," III.iv.) Unless he recaptured "the pitch of the house" at the start of the evening, he could not be secure in the rest of the rehearsal.

The director instructed the technicians to check the level of the air conditioners, to make sure that all exit doors to the house and backstage were closed. Meanwhile, Actor B walked about the stage, repeating "To be . . . to be . . . to be," at different levels until, with the shy smile of a child who had found a lost toy, he was satisfied. "Thank you very much. I've got it now. Sorry."

Prior to this interruption of the action, there was no evidence that Actor B was preoccupied with his lost pitch. His playing of the first moment was filled with authority and complexity. Like Gielgud, he was able to maintain the integrity of the observing portion of his ego at no sacrifice to the performance. I shall have occasion to return to Actor B in a later chapter; he suffers from severe stage fright.

These three examples illustrate yet another obvious, but important point: the rehearsing-actor experiences greater freedom. A rehearsal can be stopped, either by the director or the actor. You can do it over. A performance, by contrast, must inexorably keep going forward. Part of the craft of acting is to find the same freedom of expression during performance that existed in the rehearsals. Actor B, who had lost "the pitch of the house," had the latitude to stop the dress rehearsal, but he would not have done this in front of a paying audience. There have been instances, however, of an actor stopping a performance to start a scene again. For example, Anthony Hopkins, playing the demanding part of the psychiatrist in *Equus*, stopped the show after about the first ten minutes, explaining to the audience that he had lost his concentration because of the late and noisy arrival of a rather large theater party.

Thus, the oft-quoted circus/show-biz saying, "The show must go on," takes on a slightly different meaning, a more sinister one, once we recognize the double entendre in the word, "on." If "the show must go on" applies to getting the curtain up in the face of unforeseen obstacles, then the experience is toned with gallantry, camaraderie, daredevil-try. But, if going on means "on and on and on," then a very different tone emerges: one of claustrophobia, irritation, despair, and fear. There is no exit from a performance.

The performing-actor's challenge is that he has to hide a great many things from the audience. He is actually at a disadvantage in this respect from, say, a public speaker. At a lecture the speaker interrupted herself with "I'm sorry. I skipped a sentence; I'll have to go back." She had lost her place in turning the pages of her typescript, but she was not obliged to hide this performance problem from her audience.[24]

The performing-actor cannot do this. He must hide the fact that the play has been rehearsed, that, indeed, there has been a script in existence. Actors must make the audience believe that the events they are witnessing are happening for the first time. Since the actor cannot rehearse spontaneity, nor simulate it, nor calculate it, there must be some aspect of the performance each night which is actually spontaneous. While the scripted words remain the same, while the stage moves are generally reenacted, such repetitions will not come across as mechanical because they are encased in a broader framework of improvisation.

For example, many actors have been trained, or have trained themselves, to be responsive to extremely subtle variations in their partner's work. Since the actor takes nothing for granted, he does not automatically assume that his partners will deliver their lines in exactly the same way each time. In other words, the actor is presented with new stimuli at each performance which, if he is attuned to them, aid in maintaining the freshness of his own responses. "Acting is, in fact, reacting" is a phrase most actors have heard all through their training.

This aspect of improvisation is usually part of the actor's basic training and, as we have seen, governs a great deal of his rehearsal work. Even actors not necessarily associated with the Stanislavski school are aware of this crucial performance problem. Sybil Thorndike, for one, has said that the character is "newly created with each performance. It may be, and most frequently is, that the actors choose the same outward signs and movements—vocal or otherwise—at each performance. But these must be freshly selected and born at the moment and not just copies of those previous performances" (1932, p. 301).

But there is something else that the actor must hide. When the "fourth wall" rises (i.e., the curtain, either a literal one or, more frequently these days, the lights coming up on the action), the actor cannot give the impression that he is aware of the audience's existence; this would interfere with the illusion he attempts to create. As we have just seem, however, one part of the actor must remain in touch with his audience, if only to deal with such pragmatic things as timing laughs (Gielgud's tea cup), adjusting vocal levels and intonations (Actor B's "pitch of the house" problem), extending a pause in the action, or finding the exact position where certain key stage lights have been focused. A performance is a continual secret interplay, at many different levels, between actor and audience and Otis Skinner highlights the paradox of such an interplay: "Acting is not a one-sided affair. It is a collaboration between actor and audience that makes for cohesion and unity, and it is the business of the actor's art *to keep this partnership a secret to himself.* Too open an avowal of it defeats his aims and breaks the connection" (1938, p. 281, italics added). The actor's aim is defeated by "too open an avowal" of his need for the audience and also of his awareness of their existence.

Even when performing in a presentational play, where

the audience's existence is acknowledged in the form of direct address, that is, soliloquies and asides, the actor must hide from the audience his need for their approval. Furthermore, in such plays, Shakespeare being our prime example, the actor has the additional challenge of moving back and forth between scenes in which the illusion of reality depends upon a "slice of life" convention and moments of direct confrontation with the spectator. This, by the way, is one of the things that makes the acting of Shakespeare so difficult.[25]

Performing, then, is filled with contradictions. The actor must hide almost as much as he shows. He must hide things from the audience but, more important, he must hide things from parts of himself. That the play has been rehearsed, that the audience is there, for example, are secrets that must be kept from the character that the actor is portraying; the actor cannot permit his performing ego to acknowledge their existence. In addition, he must also hide his self-observing ego from the audience in order to maintain the illusion of the play. The actor (i.e., his observing ego) wants his audience only to see his performing ego; he cannot let the audience know that he is timing laughs, looking for the "hot spot," monitoring their responses, or awaiting their approval.

3

STAGE FRIGHT

I would not want even an enemy to suffer those terrible moments.
—Luciano Pavarotti

"A single note off key"

Edward R. Murrow called it "the sweat of perfection." Most actors accept it as an occupational hazard, something to be gotten rid of, to be gotten over. In *The Presentation of Self in Everyday Life*, Erving Goffman says that "a single note off key can disrupt the tone of an entire performance" (p. 52) and that audiences are particularly adept at "piercing an individual's effort at calculated unintentionality" (p. 9). Actors believe that stage fright itself is that "single note off key" that can destroy all their efforts at creating a "calculated unintentionality."

Because the performance is filled with contradictions, it is also filled with risk. This is the domain of stage fright. The actor is painfully aware that appearing in front of an audience is a scary proposition. Maintaining the reality of the character is, in itself, a very fragile affair; it demands of the actor a series of highly complex, intrapsychic transformations. As we have seen, there is the unique problem of the performing-actor: hiding and showing at the same time. The actor's conscious fear is not that he will make a mistake but that the audience will see something it is not supposed to see, namely, his fear, his stage fright.

There are endless stories about performances, and even careers, ruined by stage fright. Most working actors know, for example, that Actor B, who could not find "the pitch of the house," consumed half a bottle of gin before curtain time. A colleague of his said, "It killed his stage fright and his acting at the same time." In certain instances, actors have had to abandon the stage for radio, film, or television because they could not tolerate stage fright.[1] Actor Y, now a dependable film actor, left the stage because he had to miss performances on account of his fear: "It wasn't the stage fright that got me; it was the fear of having to go through all that crap before the curtain." Actor Y developed a "stage phobia"; he avoided the anxiety by restricting his work to films. Actor Y also made it clear that his move to film work was not because of the higher salaries. He would still like to go back to the stage, but knows he never can.

One of the most confusing and frightening aspects of stage fright is that it does not seem to go away, even after years of experience or the hundredth performance of a play, although in this latter instance, it certainly diminishes in intensity for most actors. But why should a professional actor, often playing a familiar role, still experience any stage fright at all, much less such a severe attack, as to justify the following examples?

A British actor in his late sixties still becomes so nervous before each performance that he must be dressed and made up by an assistant. First of all, his body is so out of control that he is unable to perform these functions for himself. Second of all, left to his own devices, he often forgets what play he's in and will sometimes appear costumed for another piece in the repertory. An American actress throws up before going on stage; buckets have to be placed by each of her entrance positions. Another actress, who has played many leading roles, says, "Most people are really very frightened. Getting out there on stage is like walking a tightrope. It's like walking on stage naked—naked and looking awful."

Laurence Olivier has written quite eloquently about his experiences with this debilitating occupational hazard, which actually surfaced late in his career, during the run of *The Master Builder*. Contemplating his "guilt complex" because of his "overblown claim to pride," Olivier felt that "such punishment was now served upon me in the form of a much-dreaded terror which was, in fact, nothing other than a merciless attack of stage fright with all its usual shattering symptoms." He felt he "was guilty of harboring despising thoughts" and the attack began "between the dress rehearsal and our first performance" (Olivier 1982, p. 261):

> My courage sank, and with each succeeding minute it became less possible to resist this horror. My cue came, and on I went to that stage where I knew with grim certainty I would not be capable of remaining more than a few minutes . . . I took one pace forward and stopped abruptly. My voice had started to fade, my throat closed up and the audience was beginning to go giddily round (why is it always anticlockwise?) when with a sickening feeling I realized that Noel [Coward] was in front, and would inevitably write me off into a wasteland as he had Edith [Evans].

In fact, Olivier feared that his stage fright "would mean a mystifying and scandalously sudden retirement." His anxiety attacks continued for five years and, to his increasing horror and helplessness, he saw it invade all the other roles he played. His experience in *Othello* focuses on the fear of being alone, on the need for a comforting alter ego: "I had to beg my Iago, Frank Finlay, not to leave the stage when I had to be left alone for a soliloquy, but to stay in the wings downstage where I could see him, since *I feared I might not be able to stay there in front of the audience by myself*" (p. 262, italics added). Finally, Olivier consulted with friends, Sir Lewis Casson and his wife, Dame Sybil Thorndike. She replied, "Take drugs, darling, we do."

Richard Burton sweated and shook: "When I played my first performance [in *Equus*], I was terrified I'd lost the ability to command" (1976). Paul Lynde was very outspoken. "I have never gotten over being terrified in front of an audience. Oh, I know most performers get the jitters before they go on. My reaction is more like *nervous collapse*" (cited in Bradley 1967, p. 32). Lynn Fontanne said, "Any actor who claims he's not frightened on opening nights just isn't telling the truth." Or, Estelle Parsons: "I get this feeling that I just can't go on. And sometimes I've had to stay in bed all day in order to get to the stage." Or, Gertrude Lawrence: "These attacks of nerves seem to grow worse with the passing of the years. It's inexplicable and horrible and something you'd think you'd grow out of, not into" (P. Funke 1982, pp. 6 ff.).

The examples multiply, each one attesting to a different aspect of stage fright, but one of the most complete descriptions of it comes from Maureen Stapleton (1960). I will quote her at length in order to demonstrate the intensity and variety of the symptomatology.

> When I work, it starts about six-thirty at night. I start to burp. I belch—almost non-stop. I keep burping, all through the show, right up to the curtain, and right after, and then I'm all right . . . If a truck backfires, I jump. I can hear everything. I get scared . . . And, a plane—those jets—all that noise. It terrifies me . . . I get scared that something is going to fall down, or there's going to be an explosion . . . Everybody's got a problem and I'm stuck with this. The other night I was in the dressing room when a light bulb exploded. It sounded like a cannon. I don't know what happened, it popped or something. It was a terribly loud sound. Well, I leaped up, and some of the others in the company came running down. They knew that I might faint out of absolute terror. And I did almost faint . . . I black out. I get so nervous that I can't remember what happened . . . I'm always like an automaton, opening night. The pressures are just too much . . . I'm nervous every night, but opening night is more of a nightmare . . . There's so much at stake that it just overpowers you. [Pp. 95 ff.]

George C. Scott, who acted with Stapleton in *Plaza Suite*, confirms her own description:

> She's the kind of actress who will come to the theater eight times a week and get in the wings and her heart will palpitate, she'll sweat, she will become faint, she will say, "I can't go on tonight." And you will say, "It's all right, honey, you'll be all right." Now you expect that she will barely make it, right? She hits the stage and its gangbusters, like Gibraltar, for two hours

and fifteen minutes. She comes off and "I don't know how I made it." It's just incredible. The same thing over and over and over. [Cited in Probst 1975, p. 83]

This is the well-known, uncontrollable anxiety attack in its fullest form. Yet actors like Olivier, Burton, Parsons, Fontanne, and Stapleton manage to overcome their anxiety. Experiences such as these led Donald Kaplan, a psychoanalyst who has devoted much time and attention to aspects of performance, to characterize stage fright as "a creative problem which the performing artist attempts to solve along with other problems of artistic performance" (1969, p. 60). Ultimately, our examination of how stage fright stops will help to elucidate why it starts and, more important, why Kaplan is correct in his assertion that stage fright must accompany all fine acting.

When questioned about stage fright, actors invariably reply, "It'll interfere with my performance." This appears to have very little to do with things that can actually go wrong on stage. Forgetting lines, skipping to a later section of dialogue, entering too late or too early, are happenings with which actors are trained to deal. For example, on the opening night of *Othello* at the Royal Shakespeare Company, John Gielgud, in the title role, began to lose his beard in full view of the audience. After making several attempts to stick it back onto his face more firmly, he simply ripped the whole thing off and went through the rest of the act clean-shaven. The Hamlet who lost his sword in the duel scene with Laertes transformed his entire right arm into a sword, completing the action with gusto.

In fact, actors often entertain each other with stories of how they covered up potential bloopers or invented new stage action until they could conveniently get a prompt from the stage manager. The ad-lib, for example, is relatively easy to use in prose drama but more problematic in verse. Many years ago, some members of the Royal Shakespeare Company devised an informal iambic pentameter ad-lib, "Couch we awhile, and mark," taken from *Hamlet*, V.i.209. Not only does it scan, but it also applies to almost any situation in Shakespeare.

Actors seem to understand that such mistakes rarely have any lasting impact on the audience's involvement in

the play. For the actor, they are irritating and frustrating but
they can be fixed. They are completely within the actor's
control.

It is, however, the loss of control, implicit in the helplessness and mystery of stage fright, that is consciously most
disturbing to the actor. He has had ample opportunity to
watch or hear about its overt destructiveness, but he is
never sure when and how it will manifest itself in his own
performance. Opera singers can hit a wrong note; ball players strike out, but actors fail in subtler ways: "It just didn't
feel right." Since the actor is not sure what the "it" is all
about, he can think of no effective way of combating it.

Stage fright, then, threatens to destroy performances,
forces fine actors to leave the stage and does not remit even
after years of experience. As the stage fright attack intensifies in the minutes before curtain, the actor's most common fear is that it will be communicated to the public, that it
will interfere with the illusion of the play, that it will show.
Once this happens, the actor is unmasked. The audience
has discovered his "dark, entrusted, inside or strategic secrets" (Goffman 1959, p. 235); put simply, and colloquially,
the actor's cover has been blown. As Goffman goes on to
suggest, the audience assumes that "signs of nervousness
in most cases are an aspect of the individual who presents a
character and not an aspect of the character he projects.
[The audience sees] an image of the man behind the mask"
(p. 212)—"a solitary player involved in a harried concern for
his production; a single look, a naked, unsocialized look, a
look of concentration, a look of one who is privately engaged in a difficult, treacherous task" (p. 235).

Actors will speak about themselves in much the same
way. Little and Cantor (1970) have captured the essence of
the performing-actor's subjective experience: "All the other
collaborators are in the audience or safely in the wings or in
the orchestra pit. The producer or the author or the director
may be outside having a drink—or in London. But the
actors are all alone with a thousand strangers" (p. 89);
"unassisted, exposed, alone [the actor] works in full public
view with his body, his voice, and his personality as the
direct expression of the ideas he must convey. This is why
an actor talks about how helplessly vulnerable he feels on

the stage. He is his one and only weapon, his own instrument" (p. 118).

"Exposed" and "alone with a thousand strangers"—these are the two most common themes in the actor's experience when he appears in public. The next sections will be devoted to a further exploration and elaboration of these themes, bringing us, I think, closer to an understanding of what the anxiety attack is all about, what causes it, what triggers it, what measures the actor uses to combat it, and, finally, why stage fright is a necessary component of all good acting.

A Thousand Strangers

The actor's sense of helpless vulnerability emerges in the face of his encounter with a group of people who, quite suddenly, appear on opening night. There is more than a little justification for this helplessness; its reality will now be discussed so that later on such reality issues can be separated from the actor's fantasies about the audience—fantasies that can often appear to be rampantly (paranoid) delusional.

Audiences are not particularly adept at analyzing the components of a production; they often misplace both praise and blame. Even something as seemingly direct as authorship is hard to pin down. For example, the supraordinate role of the director in the contemporary theater permits him to influence the work of the author (and the designers, for that matter) to such an extent that even someone who has followed the production process from the first day of rehearsal would have a hard time allocating praise or blame to any particular individual.

Tennessee Williams published two versions of *Cat on a Hot Tin Roof* in 1955: the first, the way he originally wrote it; the second, the way it was rewritten for Elia Kazan's Broadway production. Even a cursory examination of these texts indicates that the changes that were made resulted in two different plays. Kazan introduced what amounts to a happy ending and brought Big Daddy back in the third act. Twenty years later, Michael Kahn directed yet another version of *Cat*, retaining some of Kazan's revisions but returning to

Williams's original ending (Williams 1975; the author officially approved of Kahn's production.)

Furthermore, the casting of a play inevitably alters the audience's perception of the author's intentions. Kazan used Burl Ives; Kahn, Fred Gwynne. Leaving talent aside, the actors' vastly different (one can say "opposite") personality types, body builds, and vocal patterns definitively emphasized one or another aspect of the Big Daddy in the author's imagination. Ives captured the red-necked, jovial, raw power of the man; Gwynne, given his thin, fragile build, projected the image of a frightened man, a shell whose insides were being eaten away.

When Big Daddy's son tells him that he (Big Daddy) has cancer, this climax of the second act was so different in each case that the audience seemed to be seeing another play. "Christ-damn-all-lying sons-of-lying bitches! Yes, all liars, all liars, all lying dying liars" (Williams 1955, p. 128) was bellowed by Ives, whispered by Gwynne. These variations in turn affected the son's reactions: Ben Gazarra (with Ives) coldly watched his father's growing fear; Keir Dullea (with Gwynne) painfully regretted what he had revealed the moment he uttered the line.

The point, of course, is not to decide which version or which Big Daddy was better, but merely to demonstrate that even an apparently clear-cut issue such as authorship is very ambiguous and hard to pin down. Perhaps an even more remarkable example of how casting affects one's evaluation of a play would be the recent revival of *Death of a Salesman*. Dustin Hoffman played Willy Loman; in the original production it was Lee J. Cobb. The degree and quality of sympathy that each of these actors elicited from the audience was palpably different. Such issues as these, by the way, have led many to say that a play simply does not exist on paper; it exists only in a theater when a group of actors are confronted with an audience.

But when it comes to the actor's work, to his unique contribution, the audience's ability to evaluate the processes that led to a specific performance is truly compromised. Whose bit of business was that: the actor's, the director's, the author's, or another cast member's? Should Actor X be held responsible for the unnecessarily frenetic pace of a scene, when, in fact, it was the director who had forced him into it in order to compensate for another actor's lethargy?

Actors are indignant at being judged unfairly for elements in the production that they had nothing to do with. Marian Seldes told Little and Cantor, "I can't tell the critics, 'Look, this is the very first time I'm wearing this dress'" (1970, p. 92). And in her autobiography she gives an instance of the opposite: an actor, performing drunk on opening night, receiving rave notices (1978, p. 149). In another production, accidental noise coming from steam pipes in the theater was thought to be part of the director's production-plan, an excellent device for creating "atmosphere." In this instance, as in the ones that follow, the actors were not given their due.

Celeste Holm appeared in an out-of-town preview of a comedy directed by Michael Howard. The author had given them what he clearly intended to be a laugh line, but they could not make it work as he had written it. Left to their own devices, Howard and Holm revised only the final word in the line, changing "thief" to "crook." Once the change was made, the line worked; the audience exploded in laughter. The author got the credit, but what saved the day was the director's and actress's understanding of a basic rule of comedy. A laugh line needs to be delivered in such a way that it gives the audience permission to laugh; it has to snap them into laughter. "Thief" is not a snap word. It ends in a soft consonant; the "f" sound moves slowly and unimpressively out into the house. "Crook," on the other hand, ends with the sharp clap of the "k" and immediately commands the audience's attention, signaling them to laugh.[2]

In more than a few cases, a production has been successfully received by both critics and audiences while, unknown to any except those most closely connected with the work, the director had made almost no contribution at all. A recent Broadway smash hit, where the critics actually praised the director for his good work, became a hit in spite of him. During the out-of-town tryouts, the director was asked to leave town, in other words, to leave the actors alone. His comments were either of no help at all or actually destructive. Some actors resented the good reviews he got because it meant to them that he would soon be rehired and his lack of talent inflicted on yet another set of actors.

A final example: an actor had invented a piece of business. He hit the naked light bulb, hanging over the set, so that it swung back and forth, creating eerie shadows as the stage lights faded and the final curtain fell. But the director was the one who received the misplaced praise for creating an indelible image of death and destruction, based undoubtedly, as many critics remarked, on Picasso's *Guernica*.

It is crucial to see the issue of misplaced praise and blame in a realistic light because it forms a backdrop to the potential for "aggressive combat between the performer and the audience" (Flugel 1938, p. 189). Until it can somehow be dominated, the actor experiences impotence in front of this crowd of a thousand strangers. Many commentators on the performance process have picked up both the aggressive as well as the erotic components in the actor-audience relationship. "A child seeking to please his parents, a lover wooing his mistress, a soldier going into battle" is the way Little and Cantor put it (1970, p. 90). But, perhaps, the clearest expression of the aggressive oedipal wish comes from Burgess Meredith: "The audience is the dragon to be slain, the woman to be raped" (1970, p. 90).

The actor experiences the audience as a force to be tamed. Richard Burton's fantasy of a perfect audience was "sheep" (1976, p. 10). There is a kernel of truth in such fantasies. An audience, at the start of an evening, is often experienced from the stage as a heterogeneous unit that has to be welded together into a unified entity. The audience, composed of a thousand different people, each concerned with business or home problems, the baby-sitter, the cost of the evening out, the bloated feeling in the stomach, not to mention their expectations about being entertained, must be made to forget all these things and focus their complete attention on the stage. Audiences mirror processes that are central to the actor's work. They must temporarily diminish the investment in their own (self-)observing egos, displacing this energy onto its participating counterpart in order to enter into the action of the play. Just like actors, audiences have to become less self-conscious.

Actors speak of needing to gain "control" and "power"

over the audience. This need to control is both adaptive and defensive. The actor faces the pragmatic necessity of commanding the audience's attention as a precondition for the performance to take place. But the (excessive) need to control is often based upon the actor's fear that something inside himself will get out of control; he has fears about "messing up" and overacting, that is, becoming too excited.

Cornelia Otis Skinner, primarily a comedienne, experienced severe stage fright. Speaking quite seriously, she said her fear was that she "might suddenly go mad and goose the leading man or walk calmly up to the footlights and stick out [her] tongue at Brooks Atkinson" (Moramarco 1976, p. 6). To "go mad" is the feared loss of control, and it is interesting to note the regressive form that her madness might take: a playful assault on a male figure on stage and a calm, almost premeditated, little girl's challenge to a male authority figure in the audience. Cornelia Otis Skinner's father was the famous American actor quoted earlier. He was her "leading man" and her Brooks Atkinson critic-mentor all through her life.

In fact, as Goffman (1959) points out, the numerous practical jokes actors play on each other, to make their partners "crack-up" on stage, are designed to reassure each of them that "he has this interaction so much under control that he can toy with it at will" (p. 189). I would only add that these jokes often seem to be sexual in nature and very risky, indeed. Actress X once appeared in a play in which a bereaved widow (actually her husband's murderess) must stand silently over his coffin for a very long time. To amuse herself, possibly to combat boredom, Actress X nightly zipped and unzipped her partner's fly. Because of the staging, the audience could not see this bit of business. The actor eventually replied; one night as X continued her ritual, she saw that he had drawn a large arrow in red lipstick pointing downward. Apparently, she collapsed in laughter and almost fell over the coffin. However, what the audience saw that evening was the widow convulsed in tears, sobbing as she doubled over with grief.

For actors, a theater is composed of dressing rooms, a backstage area, on-stage, and the house or, as it used to be called, the hall. The dressing room is their private place; a knock on the door is usually needed to gain entry. The backstage, including the "green room" in some theaters (i.e., the lounge), is the shared space of the performance team. The house belongs to the audience. The stage, while it may seem like the actors' exclusive domain, is actually conceived of as an intermediary space, linked to the audience. A play begins with the lifting of the fourth wall, either literally, if there is a curtain, or figuratively, when lights must dissolve the initial darkness. As quickly as possible, the actors want to obliterate the audience's memory of the curtain. An important and conscious performance goal is to unite the stage and the house into one entity.

Most theaters now have an intercom system in each dressing room and in most of the backstage areas so that the actor can hear the members of the audience as they begin to take their places in the house. It is at this point that the intense nervousness known as stage fright begins. Performance has now become a psychic reality. Up to this point, it is not uncommon for frightened actors to try to comfort themselves with the thought that, for one reason or another, the audience actually will not show up that night.

The audience's arrival in the house initiates a significant process within the actor whereby he must somehow ignore their existence. This psychic task, denial, promotes unconscious elaboration of fantasies about the thing denied.[3] Denial of the audience manifests itself in different ways. It can take the form of a denial of their importance, evident in the actor's derogatory comments about them. Or, the actor thinks of them as "strangers," thereby avoiding any hint of a more personal interaction that is about to take place. But this need to deny both the existence and the significance of the house paradoxically intensifies the actor's inner sense of loneliness.

We recall that the author, producer, or director may well be out in the lobby, in the bar across the street, or in another country. "All alone with a thousand strangers" is certainly the way a performance begins for the actor, and it compels him to unite his "stage" with their "house" as well as to weld this disparate group into a unified, attentive presence. The actor is unaware that similar feelings exist within an audience, namely, each member's strangeness with regard to the person seated next to him. If the performance process reduces the distance between actor and audience, it also does exactly the same thing for each member of the audience. I suspect it is not totally coincidental that contemporary American actors enjoy quoting Blanche's exit line from *A Streetcar Named Desire*, "Whoever you are—I have always depended on the kindness of strangers" (Williams 1947, p. 165).

We must now imagine the actor in his dressing room, preparing for the performance, trying to combat stage fright, hoping to avoid its extreme symptomatology. It is not only that he begins to feel alone as the audience gathers that intensifies the stage fright attack; it is also that, having tried every conscious means at his disposal, he fails to ward off the anxiety. The actor is abandoned by his own defense mechanisms.

"There is a ritual in the dressing room," notes Marian Seldes, "private for some, gregarious for others. The look of the room, the temperature, where each article of clothing is set—yours and the character's—mementos from other plays . . . A different robe for the theater. Special towels, soap, cologne. Brushes and combs. The actual tubes or sticks of makeup, the brushes" (1978, p. 145). Terry Kiser echoes Seldes: "When I get to my dressing room, I do the same thing every night. I always have a cup of coffee. I shine my shoes. I put on cologne for freshness. I shave at the theater. I wash my hair every day. My hair tends to be greasy. I like it fluffed up. It gives me a different look. I always go on stage before the curtain" (Little and Cantor 1970, p. 93). Kiser's dressing room has become a second home for him; this helps to diminish the fears about losing "the house," which, at the present moment, is occupied by strange interlopers.

The simple act of going over the lines of the play offered Vivien Leigh relief (Funke and Booth 1963, p. 89), as it did Ruth Gordon, who "invariably paces in the wings like a caged lioness, waiting for show time, muttering to herself; she is going over her lines, which she repeats to herself every night of the run in the same methodical restlessness" (Little and Cantor 1970, p. 111). This is not a question of review in order to remember the lines, but rather a ritualistic attempt at self-comfort. By repeating words devoid of meaning, the actor creates a kind of litany, which at once distracts him from the here-and-now and puts him magically in touch with an image of a stable, unchanging text.

Other actors try to work off their anxiety through physical means. Actress E jumps up and down on the couch in her dressing room in an attempt to "wear out that demon inside me." Frederic March, who suffered severe stage fright at every performance, regularly did "ten minutes of vocal exercises prior to his entrance, humming and articulating" (Little and Cantor 1970, p. 93). None of these coping mechanisms are effective. (For another example, see below p. 92.)

We have already seen that actors work within a regressive context during rehearsals; it should not surprise us to learn that the actor's backstage behavior has its own regressive character. In fact, almost any kind of behavior is tolerated by other cast and crew members. In general, actors attempt to cope with their anxiety by maintaining a fixed routine upon entering the theater, a routine that can become so obsessively ritualized that if one element is out of order, the anxiety immediately intensifies.

Goffman has noted that the varieties of backstage behavior include

> Reciprocal first-naming, co-operative decision-making, profanity, open sexual remarks, elaborate griping, smoking, rough informal dress, "sloppy" sitting and standing posture, use of dialect or substandard speech, mumbling and shouting, playful aggressivity and "kidding," inconsiderateness for the other in minor but potentially symbolic acts, minor physical self-involvements such as humming, whistling, chewing, nibbling, belching, and flatulence . . . Backstage behavior has what psychologists might call a "regressive character." [P. 128]

In fact, he defines backstage as a place which "gives individuals an opportunity to regress . . . to feel that it is safe to lapse into an asociable mood of sullen, silent irritability" (1959, p. 132).

Often, however, the irritability is not silent. Direct expression of aggression toward the audience is another means to which actors consciously resort in order to diminish their stage fright. "Knock 'em dead," "Lay 'em out in the aisles," and "Let's cream 'em" are phrases frequently heard on opening night. Actor Q wants "to fuck the audience up the ass"; he claims that it is only by mobilizing such a high degree of sadistic energy that he can actually get himself out on the stage each night. Laurence Olivier used to stand behind the curtain, muttering "You bastards" at the audience over and over again, while Blythe Danner buoys up her self-confidence with a kind of battle-cry, "Go out there and maim them" (Little and Cantor 1970, p. 92). Actors under normal circumstances tend to divide their universe into the Runyonesque communities of "citizens" (the public) and "gypsies," so that the derogatory remarks just before a performance not only maintain this adversarial relationship. They are also attempts at creating a sense of control over the "bad audience" by giving it a name. Like the methodical repetition of their lines or a physical task, however, such statements of aggressive insult rarely succeed.

Directors invariably convene the cast for a few hours on opening day to give the actors a chance to work off their nerves and reduce the lonely isolation before performance. A run-through, a line rehearsal, even an extended improvisation, is arranged, but Seldes describes a rather untypical day: "[Anthony] Hopkins could imitate other actors brilliantly. It was a shock and surprise to me when Dexter [the director of *Equus*] urged him to do Dysart's part as Brando, as Burton, as Gielgud, as Humphrey Bogart, at the final rehearsal on the day we opened. A way of loosening tensions? A waste of a rehearsal? The naughty children laughed" (1978, p. 196).

Occasionally, an entire cast will get together on their own. The original company of *Fiddler on the Roof* was an example. "When 'Places!' is called just before the curtain, all cast members go out on stage and circulate quietly. The ceremony, which began spontaneously soon after the show opened, strengthened friendship and communal spirit and is akin to a religious ritual" (Little and Cantor 1970, p. 113).

In part, this may have been an attempt to reduce the sense of individual isolation.

In less formal ways, the group will attempt to master what the individual cannot. Before the curtain, actors sometimes exchange stories about past performances, recalling famous "show-biz bloopers." This is usually an effort to give historical authenticity to stage fright as a phenomenon that has been and, therefore, can be overcome. Gabbard correctly notes that before a performance, "the experience of stage fright is seldom alluded to, as if the mere mention of it will cause the reaction to intensify" (1979, p. 383). But in recalling ways in which other actors have dealt with technical problems, fooling the audience into believing that all was well, there is a modest allusion to the not-to-be-spoken-of topic. For instance, a story, which made the rounds for several years, concerned John Gielgud, playing Wolsey in *Henry VIII*. One night, he completely forgot his lines but recovered magnificently by stringing together, with great authority, disconnected lines from Shakespeare: "O, what a rogue and peasant slave am I / Made glorious summer by this sun of York."

Such group efforts are usually of little value in containing the approaching anxiety attack. Each actor seems ineluctably drawn back into himself. Some have been known to arrive at the theater literally minutes before the curtain. They rush into costume and makeup, entering on cue with not a moment to lose. Presumably, they avoid the entire preperformance ritual in the theater as a way of denying, until the last possible moment, that they will have to go on that night.

Unlike other performance teams, a cast is not much help to its individual members when it comes to reducing the stress of stage fright. But, then again, a cast differs from most all other performance teams in one important respect: it becomes a leaderless group directly after the final dress rehearsal. Furthermore, during its performance, the cast of a play receives no coaching from the sidelines. Once the performance begins, the actor is truly on his own. In 1921 Freud examined the kinds of anxieties that can arise under the condition of a leaderless group, with particular reference to the emergence of aggression, often in the form of xenophobia—an aggression that had heretofore been bound by the presence of the leader. He also noted that groups of this kind tend to exhibit regressive behavior as well.

This issue of the leaderless group is a complex one. Stage managers have often had to ask—and sometimes order—directors to leave the backstage area because their presence was unnerving: it heightens the ambivalence within the cast. On the one hand, the actor needs to feel autonomous with regard to his performance; he has to dare to engage in the process of creating a character on his own. On the other hand, the actor deeply wishes for the benevolent presence of the director. Sometimes he tries to persuade himself that the performance will be all right, if it can be made to seem just like another rehearsal. The situation is akin to a young child's first day at school. Often, mother's presence unnerves the child by exerting a regressive pull which is too potent to overcome. Finally, of course, if the actor were to catch sight of the director, it might pull him out of the imaginary circumstances of the play, not to mention the other obvious fact that the director's own anxiety could communicate itself to the cast.

But by far the most common attempt at coping with the emerging anxiety is to try to immerse oneself in the given circumstances of the play as the first step in the transformation from actor to character. This preparation must be done alone. Of course, preperformance preparation is considered by many actors to be essential under any conditions, but all of them hope that such work will also reduce the anxiety. Paradoxically, then, many actors prefer to remain alone at the very moment when they begin to fear the state of "aloneness."

This preparation can take many forms. Without resorting to any of the specific details of the play, that is to say, ignoring what is about to happen in the character's life, the actor will often focus on such character-oriented questions as Where am I coming from? What aspirations do I have? What are my expectations about what might happen after I get off that streetcar named "Desire" at the stop called "Elysian Fields"? In short, the first justification is the most important justification; it forces the actor-character to con-

sider what circumstances in his life have made the first
entrance inevitable. The idea here is that once the actor is on
stage and responsive to the stimuli produced by the other
characters as well as by his own inner imaginative processes, matters will take care of themselves.

Preparation need not take this intellectual form. Actors
use a variety of techniques to bring themselves into the life
of the play. Some put on makeup and costume at once,
using their reflected images as the initial source of inspiration. Others will carefully examine their props, for example,
a pocket watch (Ben in *Death of a Salesman*), a set of keys
(Varya in *The Cherry Orchard*), an embroidered handkerchief
(Desdemona in *Othello*).

Still others find that activation of any of the senses,
particularly the sense of smell, is useful. In addition, music,
a book of poems, some piece of food with specific meaning
to the character perform similar functions. In general, such
sensory stimuli may be so powerful for the actor that they
immediately open up to him the entire imaginative world of
the play. Psychologists, particularly those who use imaging
as part of a behavior modification regime, and psychotherapists, who pay special attention, for example, to the most
vivid sensory image in the manifest dream content, are
familiar with the evocative power of such releasing-stimuli.

The assumption here is that by the time the actor reaches
the stage, he will be so deeply involved in the given circumstances of the play that the audience will be less important to him, that "the black hole" of the proscenium, as
Stanislavski used to call it (1936, p. 10), will no longer exert
its strong pull. This is made possible by the actor's skill in
the use of sense memory and emotion memory as adjuncts
in advancing what we might call an adaptive regression in
the service of the performing ego. As a matter of fact, much
of contemporary acting training has to do with exercises
designed to promote this process of the overinvestment of
psychic energy in specific self-images. Students, for instance, become adept at recalling their favorite toy. They are
immediately impressed by the power of such a memory
because, in addition to the recall of the toy, they find they
are flooded with associated memories and the affective
states linked to them. Needless to say, exercises in relaxa-

tion and concentration must precede and continually accompany such work.

This type of preparation does not significantly diminish the anxiety. Although it attempts to insure that the play inside the actor's head has become more important than the events that are actually taking place in the external world of the opening night, it cannot reverse the regression. In fact, as we shall see, this kind of profound immersion in the circumstances of the play and the character's life is one of the prime causes of stage fright.[4]

"Places, please!" ushers in the final phase of the anxiety attack; the curtain is about to rise; the audience is almost seated. Communication between the house manager and the stage manager determines the actual moment when the stage manager will give his first cue, usually to the electrician: "House to half, please." The house lights are dimmed to urge latecomers into their seats. Once the audience has sufficiently settled and the house manager is in control of the lobby, he makes his final contact with the stage manager, "Ok! Take it away. It's all yours." The world of backstage, including the curtained stage area, has been taken away, disconnected, momentarily isolated from the house.

Actors in the wings can hear such communiqués and the language that a stage manager uses to "call" a show may also have an impact on the cast. The next series of cues come rather quickly: "House out! Music [cue number] one, go! Warn electrics one! Warn sound one! Warn curtain!" And then, "Electrics one, sound one, . . . go! . . . And, curtain!" At the peak of their anxiety, some actors find themselves uncannily susceptible to words like "warning," "electrics," and "house out," with its unconscious registration of the fact that a potentially safe place, a home that could be filled with friends and not strangers, has been obliterated. In addition, the stage manager's forceful, often clipped, repetitive use of the word "Go!" implies that there is no turning back and that what has to be produced by the actor must be produced now.

Actors experience the peak of their anxiety during the agonizing wait between "Places!" and "Curtain!" They have lost a sense of time; what may, in fact, take no more than five minutes, can seem like an eternity. "When I begin to move toward the stage, I'm in limbo" (Actor E). The actor is trapped, literally and figuratively. "Places!" orders him to remain still and silent, while "Curtain!" suggests that hidden thoughts and actions are about to be revealed to thousands of public eyes.

Time has stopped for the actor. He is neither off stage nor on; he is somewhere between himself and the character, and, unconsciously, he can associate "house out" with the accomplishment of his destructive wishes toward the audience. In other words, repressed impulses are now, as it were, very close to the surface, pressing for discharge in action. It is precisely at this point that many actors feel the urge to flee, to escape. They envy the author and director their freedom. This envy often takes the form of an angry resentment toward the director, further intensifying the actor's sense of isolation.

In these five minutes, which on some opening nights can stretch to fifteen, the actor feels "trapped," "constricted," and "claustrophobic." "A staggering element in stage fright," Kaplan says, is that the *"performance deprives the performer of recourse to the hand and postural system"* (1969, p. 69; Kaplan's emphasis). This is to say, the actor's "personal style of achieving poise is disallowed by the requirements of performance" that is, the characterization (p. 70).

The implications of such a loss of "recourse to the hand and postural system" are very great. When people attend public gatherings like cocktail parties, business meetings, and weddings, objects like cigarettes, drinks, candies, and pads and pencils are always available as an acceptable means to reduce the tension of group encounters, to maintain the sense of individual poise. Clothing also plays a significant part here: pockets can hide cold, tremorous hands; purses can anchor impulsive gestures. Such "unmeant gestures," as Goffman calls them, are momentary lapses in muscular control (akin to Kaplan's "postural system") and would include tripping, stumbling, belching, yawning, stuttering, as well as urges "to scratch . . . or be flatulent" (1959, p. 52).

The actor, however, is forced to suppress all such coping mechanisms, ones that would normally be available to him under other circumstances of public appearance. What is more, the actor hopes that his involuntary, motor discharges will somehow be suppressed insofar as they are contrary to the behavior of the character he is trying to create. Actress A, for instance, fears that the audience will see the sweat under her armpits, particularly when her costume includes a light, silky blouse.[5]

Thus, the stage manager's call for "Places!" resonates within the actor as a literal command to "stand still in place" and to stop all activity that he had previously instituted to comfort himself. British stage managers call "Beginners, please." While the message is the same, this command troubles some actors because they hear it as a blow to their narcissism. "I've always hated that bloody call. The last thing I want to be reminded of when going on stage is that I might still be a 'beginner.' Besides, it sounds like he's talking to children" (Actor A).

If flight is impossible, then the call for "places" makes fight inoperative, too. Consciously, the actor tries to inhibit his voluntary coping mechanisms and "unmeant gestures;" unconsciously, the ego's defensive maneuvers are compromised to such an extent that the actor enters a state of panic anxiety. It is this particular kind of immobility, where the actor's usual repertoire of self-comforting gestures are "disallowed by the requirements of performance," which is central to the traumatic nature of stage fright. In the seconds before he must act, the performer is rendered passive.

4

TRAUMATIC ANXIETY

I wouldn't give a nickel for an actor who isn't nervous.
—David Belasco

A Match in a Barrel of Gunpowder

The actor has now reached the final phase of the stage fright attack. He is waiting in the wings for his cue to enter and we would do well to wait for a moment, too.

Stage fright is a severe anxiety attack, a form of panic anxiety; it is sometimes called traumatic, disintegration, or primal anxiety. For reasons that will become apparent later on, Kaplan (1969) is correct when he calls it "morbid." These labels—panic, traumatic, disintegration, primal, morbid—are used to differentiate such subjectively experienced anxiety attacks from another important concept, namely, signal anxiety, which functions silently and efficiently and is a part of everyday life. In fact, it is the breakdown of the capacity to generate appropriate signal anxiety that particularly characterizes stage fright.

In normal functioning, signal anxiety, in the face of an external or internal (intrapsychic) threat, compels the ego to institute a set of defensive measures that help restore psychic equilibrium. Essentially, confronted with an external danger, the individual can resort either to fight or flight. But, if the danger which threatens comes from within the mind itself, then actual fight or flight is not possible. It is here that the ego must resort to the mobilization of intrapsychic coping mechanisms, the defenses, of which, perhaps, repression is the most familiar.

As Anna Freud pointed out long ago (1936), we rarely have an opportunity to study these mechanisms in operation, precisely because, when the psychic apparatus is functioning under normal circumstances, such processes occur invisibly. In other words, the mind attempts to maintain a continual state of dynamic equilibrium and it is only when the ego comes into serious conflict with repressed wishes driving for gratification, with conscience, and with the demands of the external world that such ego functions as signal anxiety and the defenses become more apparent. We then see "the mind in conflict" (Brenner 1982). Of course, these mechanisms can also be inferred from ordinary mental events such as dreams, slips of the tongue, and even jokes (Freud 1901 1905).

The essence of the psychological dynamics of stage fright is that signal anxiety fails to mobilize effective defenses. It is almost as if the signal has exhausted itself in the same sense that a ship's radio operator wearies of sending out a continuous, unanswered SOS. As the actor consciously tries to suppress all "unmeant gestures" and so loses his access to self-comforting motility, to his "personal style of achieving poise," signal anxiety finally sets off what it normally purports to avoid, namely, the traumatic state. Fenichel's imagery is most expressive: "Major anxiety attacks . . . leave no doubt that the ego, in giving a signal, has set off something which . . . it can no longer control. . . . An 'anxiety signal' . . . often has the same effect as a match in a barrel of gunpowder" (1934, p. 303).

The actor, waiting in the wings, can resort to neither fight nor flight. He is physically and emotionally trapped, and there is an intimate relationship between such immobility and passivity on the one hand and panic anxiety on the other. Waelder (1967) saw the sensation of fear (anxiety) as "predicated upon an obstacle to motoric activity" (p. 352). He cites Federn's excellent metaphor: anxiety as "inhibited flight." Fenichel also highlights this aspect when he notes that panic anxiety sets in if the person has no opportunity to discharge the buildup of tension through a task, particu-

larly *"if one is forced to wait quietly"* (1945, p. 133; italics
added). This is the crux of the matter; this is precisely what
the actor has to do after he has been put in his place.

The restriction and alteration of motility plays a large part
in this traumatic attack; in a sense, immobility, in its
psychological form of "feeling trapped," is the "match"
that sets off the final phase of extreme symptomatology.
Certain repetitive dreams that actors report are significant
in this respect; they are striking in their similarity and
ubiquity. The content of such dreams seems to find its
manifest source in this final phase of the attack since they
portray, in nightmare form, things like loss of rehearsed
function, loss of control, spatial disorientation, deper-
sonalization (Stapleton's "automaton" feeling), and blocking (Kaplan 1969, p. 64).[1]

Such dreams contain the following elements in various
combinations. The actor dreams he is on stage, ready to say
his lines, but no sound comes out. The actor cannot remember his lines. The actor, on stage, fully costumed, discovers
to his horror and dismay that he is in the wrong play, not
the one for which he rehearsed. (This dream, by the way,
was not had by the actor referred to earlier, who actually did
put on the wrong costume because of his preperformance
nerves.) The actor is on stage, he can't move, he is struck
dumb; and finally, the actor is performing in a theater which
is much too large for him, for example, Radio City Music
Hall.

The governing affect associated with the content of these
nightmares is almost always "a feeling of being trapped."
These dreams are random occurrences in the overall dream
life of the actor, although through further investigation, one
could undoubtedly determine their day residues, that is,
the here-and-now catalyst that triggers the dream. They do
not seem to increase in frequency as an opening night
approaches. Such dreams, however, are repeating the actor's experience during the traumatic phase; this is similar
to what Freud (1920) observed in soldiers who had returned
from World War I. It was his examination of the traumatic
neuroses that led him beyond the pleasure principle to the
concept of a repetition compulsion. The actor's dream-life
exhibits a similar need to repeat the traumatic state in order

to master it. Finally, the symptoms in these dreams represent familiar concomitants to states of primal (panic) anxiety, particularly the helpless vulnerability.

The physical symptoms of anxiety cover a wide range of possibilities. They can include dizziness, sweating, trembling, palpitations, nausea, dryness of the mouth, diarrhea, frequent urination, muscular tension, and, of course, respiratory difficulty. But anxiety can also make itself felt through other body states: Estelle Parsons's fatigue, for instance, or Olivier's giddiness as his audience started to revolve "anticlockwise." An interesting example of how anxiety can be converted into a physical symptom comes from Helen Hayes, who often goes deaf on opening nights. "I couldn't hear a thing, except what was being said onstage" (P. Funke 1982, p. 9). Her selective deafness represented and achieved her wish to exclude the potentially threatening audience from her awareness, focusing her attention exclusively on her friendly colleagues. Ironically, her defense by conversion also prevented her from hearing the applause at the end of one opening night.

Freud pointed to the impairment of function in the "respiratory and vocal musculature" (1926, p. 137) and traced its roots to the infant's cry for help, which creates an irregular heartbeat. Some interference in the actor's normal breathing pattern is always noted during the anxiety attack; it can range from hyperventilation to an unconscious holding of the breath. Richard Burton, overcoming his anxiety on stage, said "I breathed a sigh of relief" (1976). In fact, Goffman suggests that "the crucial test of one's ability as a performer is the management of one's face and voice" (1959, p. 217).

Kaplan (1969) describes a three-phase development in the stage fright attack. An initial phase, indicating the early signs of conflict in the actor about performance, can be characterized by momentary flashes of panic, manic agitation, moods of depression, and obsessional fantasies with hypochondriacal features. When the performance becomes a psychic reality—the stage manager's "Fifteen minutes, please!"—a second phase is entered, a transient, reversible form of delusional thinking where "the audience is convening for an occasion of devastating ridicule and humiliation for the performer'' (p. 63). As the curtain is about to rise, the final phase is ushered in, culminating in ''a split between a functioning and an observing self.'' At the peak of the anxiety attack, ''the observing self perceives the functioning self as off at a distance, operating mechanically before an audience which is also perceived as quite distant'' (p. 64).

Almost every actor that I have directed or spoken with about stage fright has experienced some of the symptoms Kaplan describes. The intensity varies, however, from person to person, and, what is even more perplexing for the actor, his own particular experience with stage fright rarely remains constant from production to production or from night to night. His concern, then, is not that he will experience stage fright but that it will not be contained and that he will have to suffer through what Kaplan describes as the ''extreme symptomatology'' of the third phase.

But, if there are quantitative variations, there is qualitative stability. The content of the anxiety remains the same; even for those actors who experience stage fright as a form of free-floating anxiety, this contentless quality seems to remain constant.

Yet we have actually said nothing so far about the content of the anxiety, about what it is that frightens the actor; we have merely sketched in the dynamics of a panic anxiety attack. But the material in previous sections is suggestive of a particular avenue of investigation. Psychoanalysis has taught us that such anxiety attacks have, as it were, a developmental history; they find their ancestry in certain significant events in childhood. In other words, there are many sources of anxiety based upon developmental and maturational hurdles that the child must overcome. In this respect, we are, like detectives, or to use one of Freud's favorite images, archaeologists, engaged in an elaborate act of reconstruction.

Initially, the infant fears the loss of the mother or mothering figure. This is the earliest experience of anxiety, perhaps the most devastating, since the loss of mother would entail the loss of those life-giving supplies which she provides. Anxiety derived from this level of experience can carry with it reverberations of annihilation, a psychic death, a dissolution of the sense of self. This is often referred to, somewhat loosely, as separation anxiety.

The next phase involves fear of the loss of love. The child has now progressed to a level in development where he is able to distinguish between me and not-me, to maintain a somewhat permanent mental image of mother, but he is now vulnerable to anxiety about the withdrawal of her love and approval. This phase of development coincides with the child's toilet training so that issues of producing in a certain place at a specific time become prominent. The child's anger toward both his parents can be quite intense and in itself become a source of anxiety.

Ultimately, there emerges castration anxiety, where the fantasied punishment revolves around the oedipal triangle. The final stage in this developmental sequence is the anxiety of conscience, often called superego anxiety, more commonly talked about and experienced as guilt. It can be readily seen that this progression of anxiety-producing events follows Freud's outline of the psychosexual stages of development (1905a): the oral, anal, and phallic.

Therefore, stage fright does not have one cause, but many. Appearing before an audience revives in the actor some of these ubiquitous core conflicts from childhood, which manifest themselves in the panic attack. Gabbard notes that "the relative importance of any one conflict . . . is determined by the early childhood experience of the person under consideration" (1979, p. 385). While individual differences clearly determine which level of anxiety is initially activated during the attack, we will see that in the performing stage actor, where his talent permits and, indeed, demands a profound transformation of self into the character, a regression to the earliest phase of anxiety determination is inevitable.

And, as long as we keep Kris's important distinction between "ancestry" and "identity" in mind (1952), we will not fall into the trap of reductionistic thinking. In other words, to say that an aspect of stage fright finds its genetic determinants in castration anxiety does not mean that the attack experienced as an adult is the same as the one felt by the child. Such a statement is only meant to suggest that the same kinds of conflicts with which he had to deal as a child have been revived in the actor. Indeed, the adult has a larger array of coping mechanisms at his disposal; his ego has achieved greater structuralization so that its functions, such as judgment, memory, anticipation, capacity to delay (instinctual) gratification, and reality testing, are more acute, flexible, and resilient. Developmentally speaking, ego has expanded to include higher levels of defense, more selective, less global mechanisms.

Finally, I would ask the reader to keep in mind that, since the childhood experiences which act as prototypes for later anxiety attacks are ubiquitous, we are not in the realm of pathology. Kaplan (1969) and Weissman (1969) believe that the actor comes pretty close to it, but, in the main, the processes we are about to describe are, for lack of a better term, within normal limits. Gabbard underscores this crucial point for us when he notes that these anxiety-producing developmental hurdles are "of a *universal* nature . . . rather than only specific, pathologically distorted traumata unique to persons in the performing arts" (1979, p. 385).

Psychologists have, of course, studied stage fright, but their main concern has been with public speakers and student actors, using these populations for research protocols. Since the performance problems that face the stage actor are so different, this literature is not immediately helpful. Furthermore, dancers, singers, and musicians do not engage in a radical transformation of self during their performances, so that one must be cautious in using material from these sources. We need not disregard them entirely because there are aspects of the actor's conflicts which indeed overlap with other performing artists. But, as I hope to show, the differences far outweigh the similarities. One simple example: the singer and musician generally perform in the presence of the conductor; the dancer has direct access to the music. Even in the case of the concert soloist, the instrument upon which he plays keeps him company. Some musicians frequently create a fantasied conductor in the form, say, of an old music teacher. In each instance, the performer is not so psychologically alone as the actor and is not as vulnerable to the same kinds of abandonment fears (primal anxiety) as the actor.

The psychoanalytic literature is, on the other hand, extremely useful. Although there are only a handful of articles on stage fright, fortunately, they are all first-rate. Psychoanalysis is the investigative tool, par excellence, when it comes to an understanding of the intrapsychic dynamics of anxiety and certainly when one wants to examine what shifts take place within the actor's mind as he tries to build a character. We have already seen, I believe, the value of using psychoanalytically informed observations in organizing and explaining aspects of how the actor prepares and rehearses. We shall now apply this method to the performance process and stage fright itself.

Guilty Misdeeds

Stage fright can be looked at in two ways: first, as determined by the content of that which is being presented, and, second, as a result of the performance act itself. Most of the writers on stage fright, in both the psychological and the psychoanalytic literature, have focused on the second of these determinants, namely, anxieties deriving from the act of exhibiting oneself in public. But the first determinant cannot be ignored. It often is, however, because actors are not usually credited with the same degree of creative contribution as the author. Certainly, the vast psychoanalytic literature on artistic creativity has focused almost exclusively on the poet, novelist, playwright, painter, and composer.

And yet, the material presented in earlier chapters, specifically the degree to which an actor must personalize a role, supports the contention that, at least from the psychological standpoint, the actor's creative contribution to the play is as "primary" as the author's. Saint-Denis (1960, 1982) has demonstrated that the distinction between "the actor-interpreter" and "the actor-creator" is an artificial one; he bases his argument on the primacy of improvisation as the basic tool of the actor's trade. The point, again, is to search for the psychological truth; at some level the actor believes, indeed knows, that he is using the totality of himself in the preparation and performance of a part in such a way that entitles him to think of his work as "primary."

In brief, then, the psychoanalytic theory of creativity states that an artist's work is always to some extent a pre-sentation of certain repressed instinctual wishes. As a mat-ter of fact, Fenichel thought that what is true for the artist "is especially true for the actor" (1946, p. 356). The well-known translator of French poetry, Wallace Fowlie, talking about "the mystery of the actor," said that "a play is first con-ceived by the imagination of a poet and then incarnated in the flesh of the actor. . . . In their greatest realizations, the play has given a new life, in the presence of the public, to the subconscious life of man, to his most obscure dreams, to his dormant memory, to the child he once was, to the man he might have become" (1950, p. 7). These dreams, these dormant memories, these wishes are often guilt-laden to such an extent that the artist needs the approval of the public to lessen his inner sense of transgression, that is, the anxiety of conscience.

Now the theater is unique because, unlike other art forms, the audience is present at the very moment that the artist-actor is enaged in his process of creation/re-creation. While this situation affords the actor an opportunity for something more than just "approval" to lessen his uncon-scious sense of guilt, the conflict is intensified by the fact that in the theater *the artist "acts out" in public what the writer, for example, "thinks out" in private*. To cite Fowlie once again, "Man is an immemorial mimic. The theatre is the principal art where his conscience may be at least temporarily eased by watching on the stage depiction of his fate: his eternal restlessness in the presence of the mystery of life. The actor is the mask, the sacred magical instrument forged very early in the history of man to counteract the pain of living by transcending it" (1950, p. 11).

Through processes of identification, the audience is able to take part in the underlying (unconscious) drama and so shares in the actor's guilt.[2] This is a contemporary extension of Aristotle's psychological theory of tragedy as communal catharsis through the evocation of pity and fear (awe) at the fall of the hero. The actor-priest-scapegoat "after having withdrawn from reality into daydreaming . . . finds his way back from daydreaming to society by *inducing* an audience to participate in his guilt" (Fenichel 1946, p. 356; also, of course, see Freud's essay "Creative Writers and Day-dreaming," 1908).[3]

Many of the fifteen actors who appeared as prisoners on death row had to come to terms with their own unconscious homosexual impulses. On opening night, they experienced an intensity of stage fright new to them. Until they had received the audience's consensual validation of their efforts, they were under severe pressure. When the audience applauded at the end, the actors were being told by this response that the audience had "forgiven them" for exploring and showing the audience a portion of its own unconscious mental life. In rehearsals, the cast was surprised and shocked at the degree of sexual antagonism which developed among actors who had worked together before. Several of the fight scenes continually got out of hand; the stage manager had to referee them for quite a while. Sadomasochistic behavior was clearly evident and the director felt that part of his job was to help the cast tame such impulses so that they could be presented within the formal demands of the script. This instance clarifies the way in which the two major determinants of stage fright can operate simultaneously: both the content of the work and the performance act itself contributed to the anxiety attack.[4]

Along these lines, Nicol Williamson described his plight as follows. "When I did *Diary of a Madman*, for example, I was alone on stage during the entire play and I had to present a man who was repressed and bitter, a confirmed onanist. To perform this kind of humiliating truth is always more painfully naked than the simple act of divesting oneself of one's garments." Jacques Levy, the director of *Oh! Calcutta!*, agrees with Williamson. "I don't know why it should be braver for an actor to appear in the nude than it is for him to expose his innermost feelings, as he does all the time on the stage. After all, when you're naked you're not showing a lot" (Little and Cantor 1970, p. 301). In fact, actors who have appeared unclothed seem to experience no more stage fright than their costumed partners. Actress C, one of the first to appear nude in a Broadway production (not *Oh! Calcutta!*), found a certain protection in it. She reasoned that the audience "will be so caught on my big tits that they probably won't notice my performance at all."

Laurence Olivier's stage fright encompassed his performance as Othello. He tried to combat it by asking his Iago to stand in the wings while Othello was left alone on stage to deliver his soliloquies directly to the audience. Because Othello's jealousy and paranoia is fueled by his attachment to Cassio, an attachment which is erotically tinged, Olivier may have unconsciously feared exposing his own deeply repressed homosexual impulses. (The link between homosexuality, jealousy, and paranoia has been outlined by Freud on many occasions [1911, 1922].) Olivier-Othello needed the support of his double, his partner in crime, Iago, whose own erotic feelings toward Othello are evident.

What makes such a line of inquiry less speculative is the fact that Olivier played Iago much earlier in his career, with Ralph Richardson as Othello, under the direction of Tyrone Guthrie. Olivier and Guthrie had consulted with Ernest Jones regarding the deeper meanings of the Othello-Iago relationship. Jones, of course, had already helped Olivier in the conceptualization of the *Hamlet* film. Olivier and Guthrie were "swept away by Professor Jones's contention that Iago was subconsciously in love with Othello and had to destroy him. . . . In a reckless moment during rehearsals I threw my arms around Ralph and kissed him full on the lips." Richardson was not impressed but Olivier "had one more trick up [his] sleeve; Ralph had to fall to the ground when Othello, frenzied by Iago's goadings, is helpless in the clutches of a paroxysm. I would fall beside him and simulate an orgasm" (Olivier 1982, p. 105). Actor K also had problems with Othello because the intensity of personalization severely stressed his self-image and reactivated unwelcome personal associations.

Such examples of stage fright, intensified by the emergence of repressed erotic feelings, are common and the same can be said for aggression. The actor who was playing Willy Loman had to be controlled by the director when his body went rigid with rage. It turned out that the actor-Willy, in hitting his son, Biff, was coming too close to sadistic impulses toward his own father. Reversal is a common mode of the unconscious, of the primary process: a father hitting a son is too easily transformed into a son hitting his father. During the original production of *Marat-*

Sade, there was an unusually high turnover of cast members. Actors, who were appearing as madmen in the asylum, found that the emotional stress of playing such parts was too great to tolerate for more than about six months.

Stage fright, then, occurs when "the 'play' threatens to become 'real.' Instead of participating in the actor's guilty misdeeds, the audience may turn against him and become the representative of the punishing superego" (Fenichel 1946, p. 361). The sources of "the actor's guilty misdeeds" are to be found in the successful playing out of an "objective." This acting task demands a reactivation of repressed wishes which inevitably bring ego into conflict with the conscience, that is, superego. What makes this process so dangerous psychologically for the actor is that these reactivated repressed wishes must gain partial access to the motor apparatus in order for a performance to take place, a situation which, for example, does not occur in dreams. Therefore, the ego's defensive functions are in danger of being overwhelmed and the regression in the service of the ego, an essential part of the acting process, is in danger of turning into a more global, a more disorganized, uncontrolled regression.

This first major determinant of stage fright, namely, the conflict which the content of the part sets up within the actor, will obviously vary from person to person in terms of which specific aspect of that person's psychological past is implicated. We are now in a position to look more closely at the second set of determinants for stage fright, having to do with showing off one's inner and outer self in public.

"Break a leg!"

Actors in psychotherapy, discussing their debilitating stage fright, have voiced castration anxieties in language which is not difficult to decipher: an actor imagined that, for every part he played, he was "holding a long, thick cigar tightly clenched between his teeth for all to see and impressing everyone with his 'cool' manner"; another man felt that "they'll see that I'm really small and inadequate, that I'm deceiving them"; a female singer said, "I just freeze up when I'm out there in front of an audience. . . . They'll see a piece of me, raw, naked. . . . They'll find out that there's something lesser there—that I have nothing to show" (Gabbard 1979, p. 387). We have already heard from an actress who felt that performance was like "walking on stage naked—naked and looking awful."

Just prior to performance, an actor can get so frightened because he is about to engage in an act of exhibitionism in which he will display his genital beauty for approval. The actor is fearful that the audience will ridicule his genitals. He is exposed and risks subjecting himself to punishment for the crime of exhibitionism, namely, castration. The law of talion—an eye for an eye—is operative in the unconscious. With regard to the coping mechanisms used to defeat the increasing anxiety, several actors masturbate in their dressing rooms in order to "relax." They are aware of no significant change in their anxiety state afterwards. The fact that actors try to combat stage fright in this way—fighting fire with fire—suggests that an underlying component of the anxiety attack is sexual in nature.

Although it might seem that this genital display applies only to men, in fact it carries equal significance for women. The actress's concern about a genital deficiency has been displaced onto her entire body so that the beauty of her face, her breasts, her figure is at stake when she appears in public. At the unconscious level, however, the fear of castration, to which men allude, has been replaced in women by a confirmation of a castration which has already taken place.

Many actors are quite aware of the sexual component, of how performing pleasurably stimulates them, and, they hope, their audience. After fifteen years of appearing in featured and starring roles, an actress can still say, "I'm in a state of heightened emotional and physical awareness. My dream at the end of a performance is to be greeted at the stage door by a great stud." An unmarried actress reports that "I have what I think is a normal interest in sex, but when I'm acting, I want to be wild. And the better my acting, the more intense the feeling becomes" (Little and Cantor 1970, pp. 90, 281).

But it is not only the stimulation during the performance that promotes this sexualization, it is also the sexual opportunities open to the actor after performance that presents a challenge. "When you meet a girl off stage," commented a young actor,

> you know nothing about her, but she knows who you are and everything about you. And you can go to bed with her that night. You don't need to go hunting. . . . You bare all your feelings on the stage, and then girls come around backstage afterward, goggle-eyed housewives, college girls, teenagers. It's not a question of my taking their virginity, and it's not as if I was establishing any lasting relationship. It's just taken for granted that it's just for one night. If someone throws herself at me, I'm just not disciplined enough yet to say no. [Little and Cantor 1970, p. 281]

Here the actor feels the girl in the audience knows everything about him after she has seen him bare all his feelings; given the context, he has fantasized that he has shown this young lady his excited genital. It is no surprise to learn that he had to have prior approval of his masculinity before he could engage in intercourse: "He couldn't date a girl unless she had first seen him on the stage." At this time in his life he noted that he was disturbed by "a lack of interest in myself" (Little and Cantor 1970, p. 281).

However, the sexuality inherent in performance can also become self-defeating in a more direct way. A twenty-nine-year-old actor abruptly terminated a therapy where the chief complaint was a stage fright that was hurting his career: "When on the stage he consciously dreaded that a good performance would make the women in the audience fall in love with him" (Levinson et al. 1978, p. 829). Apparently for this actor, the narcissistic gratifications of performance backfired; he feared he was inadequate to perform successfully for these women off stage. His primary fear was then displaced onto stage acting as well.[5]

George C. Scott finds "real acting—on the stage—fraught with psychological peril. You sell your nerve fibers for money. That's just as bad as hooking on Eighth Avenue; it's the same principle. What you're doing is, you're *hustling* for money. Now, there are high-class hustlers and there are $4 hustlers" (Gelb 1977, p. 11). Scott may be aware at some level that the "psychological peril" lies in the sexualized nature of performance and so perhaps he needs to debase the whole enterprise, turning it into "hustling."

Finally, the entire process of rehearsing and performing a play has been likened to the mechanism of orgasm. When Scott describes performing as "like riding a terrific roller coaster" (Gelb 1977, p. 11), the sexual symbolism is overt. Others mirror Scott's language in such phrases as "having a ball," "turned on," and "up for it." Rehearsals are the fore-pleasure; opening night represents the release from tension, i.e., the end-pleasure. While some actors might readily accept this simile, the relief experienced during performance is clearly a release from the tension both of rehearsals and of stage fright itself.[6]

Castration anxiety includes not only fantasies about the loss of the penis but also about the loss of the penis's function, including such issues as power, potency, and effectiveness. Because a performance carries with it such a high valence of sexual energy, the actor's conscious thoughts about winning the audience over almost always mask fantasies about seducing them. This phallic-exhibitionistic component of stage fright contains within it one of the actor's commonest unconscious fantasies where playing in public is equated with making love in private. The danger is that the audience will make fun of him, of his "excited erogenous zones and their functions." It is a "dread of being exposed as a sham, of having expropriated something, of adorning oneself with borrowed plumes" (Fenichel 1946, pp. 349, 361).

The colloquial word for "failure" in the theater is "flop." The onomatopoetic meaning is clear and its ideational content is instructive. The *Oxford English Dictionary* glosses the word as follows: "the heavy dull sound produced by 'flopping'; a mass of thin mud: 'The oven where the fiery flop [molten metal] was shut up for six weeks to cool.'" Actors have other, equally revealing phrases which they apply to their failures: "we bombed," "it just laid there," and "what a mess I made tonight." The opposite of a "flop" is a "hit." *Variety*, the theater's weekly newspaper, often used "socko" and "boffo" as alternatives to "hit"; these words also carry a connotation of flatulence.[7]

The resentment at having to produce at a given time and in a particular place is another important source of stage fright. Such fantasies fearfully and angrily anticipate rejection of the repressed demand for love and approval at what is being produced and they make use of images and metaphors centered around anality. Flugel analyzed a musician who, in fact, equated showing emotion in public with defecation (1938). Gabbard tells us about "an internationally renowned concert musician who stayed off the concert stage for ten years because of the dread fear that he would accidentally expel flatus during a performance." And he reports that "the fear of urinating on himself has prompted more than one performer to leave a bottle just offstage, into which he could relieve himself just prior to entrances" (1979, p. 388).

The anxiety in this phase has to do with the loss of love. Burgess Meredith is quoted as saying, "If you're in a hit, there's so much love around, you can't stand it. And if it's a flop, the audience is merciless and there's very little you can do about it." If things are not going well, Blythe Danner gets "furious . . . I feel not liked" (Little and Cantor 1970, p. 91).

When the audience does not respond, George C. Scott is "disgusted and revolted and hurt and confused." "Disgusted and revolted" is the actor's response not only to the reality of the audience's disapproval and his own intense anger at them; what he also finds disgusting and revolting are his own unconscious fantasies about the mess that he is producing. Scott continues: "When I got into acting, it was a release for me and I have always tried to keep it separate—I've tried very, very hard. There are actors who are interested in revealing themselves, who would *smear their own hangups over any role*. I find that despicable. I can't conceive of anyone paying money to go to the theatre to look at the inner soul of any actor who ever lived" (Gelb 1977, pp. 11–12; italics added).

Such examples show us how the actor can fear that his work will be evaluated and rejected as his stool once was. "Production" is intimately linked with anal issues, as Freud first demonstrated in his *Three Essays* (1905). There he began to work out the various meanings that the child's feces have to him, for example, as penis, gift, and baby. If the actor left rehearsals with the intention of getting the director to like his work, then he begins performance with the displacement of this wish onto the audience: I want to get them to love (me for) what I've produced, the gift I'm giving them.

An American actor, in fact, found that his stage fright completely vanished the moment he was given permission to make a mess. Appearing in his first Broadway production, he recalled the opening night as one of "absolute terror." Fortunately, on his very first entrance, he was accompanied by the play's star, Menasha Skulnick. Sensing his young companion's terror, Skulnick whispered to him, "Don't worry about a thing. Tonight, everything's going to be absolutely awful."

Many of the coping mechanisms we have observed backstage, immediately prior to the performance, take the form of obsessive rituals, instituted to combat the feared loss of control. Themes of "holding in" and "letting go" can find their expression in the actor's concerns about "overacting" and "underplaying." In this regard, the bodily contents, as Flugel's patient indicated, are equated in fantasy with emotion. Such fantasies grow out of the common experience of actually feeling "empty" after the performance of a particularly "draining" part. Finally, while "Break a leg!" in America is the ubiquitous counterphobic encourgement to fellow actors, pointing, as it does, to castration anxiety, the French use "Merde!" as their morale booster. "Merde!" contains within it the thought, "Relax. It's all right to make a mess."

A Thoughtless Hunger

Common sense tells us that the actor is afraid of being looked at by the audience. In fact, actors may well have adopted masks in the ancient Greek theater in part to protect themselves from the evil eye of the spectator (Siebers 1983). Stage fright undoubtedly includes a fear of the devouring eye of the audience which, in some way, will damage him. "It occurred to me one night, while on stage and waiting for my cue, that if one looks at the two galleries in the dark, they remind one of an open mouth ready to swallow you up." This comment was made by an actor who was forced to return to radio because he was afraid of forgetting his words (Bergler 1949, p. 318). Primitive man and superstitious people are often afraid of the camera's eye because, when they have their likeness taken, they make concrete in fantasy the act of "taking" as if they might lose a bodily part or some aspect of their own personality. A common clinical example, cited by Fenichel, is a child who feared the camera and the X-ray machine for just such reasons. The "specific punishment for the exhibitionist" can take the form of a fantasy where "the eye which looks at him will bite off part of him or devour him whole" (1935, p. 396).

In a strikingly titled essay, "I Look at the Audience," Sybil Thorndike (1932) seems to suggest that she dares to look at the unlookable, as if the audience were a "Medusa's head." Sybil Thorndike's "look" indicates that something else is going on, namely, that the actor harbors fantasies about the power of his own "look"—a look so potent that it can defeat the thousand pairs of eyes focused on him. In other words, the exhibitionist is also a voyeur. Freud (1910 [1909]) noted the intimate relationship between "the active and passive desire for looking, from the former of which curiosity branches off later on and from the latter the impulsion to artistic and theatrical display" (p. 44). The voyeur fears that he will be punished by being turned into stone and the immobility implied, the stiffness in the legs, is, of course, a very common symptom of stage fright.

In the theater, the actor can cast a hypnotic spell over the audience. This "enchantment by the glance of the eye" leads "the victim" to imitate the movements and gestures of the hypnotist-magician (Fenichel 1935, pp. 374 ff.). In sharp contrast to the cinema, one continually notices that, during moments of great intensity on stage (either tragic or comic), members of the audience actually mirror the facial expressions and upper torso postures (the neck and the shoulders) of the actor.[8] The "irresistible gaze," "the enchantment by the glance of the eye," bring to mind portraits of nineteenth-century actors, for example, Keane, Booth, Macready, where the raised eyebrow and the chronic stare at colleague or audience are so apparent and so commanding. The eye as a sadistic weapon, with "to look at" equated with "to devour," often plays a part in the fantasies of both actors and spectators.[9]

In the previous section, we looked at destructive fantasies portrayed in what analysts call anal-sadistic terms: "I want to fuck the audience right up the ass" (Actor Q). The child begins to say "no" to mother and father over their demands that he produce at a certain time and in a certain place, that is, the toilet-training phase. But he has had even earlier experiences with aggression, namely, over issues surrounding feeding. The performance act evokes within the actor intense and angry conflict over who is feeding whom. On the one hand, he must maintain the idea that he is in charge of the event, feeding the audience his "good" performance. On the other, he is all too painfully aware of how much he depends on them to be fed with their applause, approval, and recognition. These oral issues become one of the most compelling sources of stage fright and we can now begin to see why the actor is so vulnerable: he must protect himself not only from the audience's devouring aggression but also from his own.

Images of feeding and being fed are commonplace in the vernacular; food and drink tend to play important parts in actor's lives. Rae Allen puts it this way: "If you don't feed your talent, it will die" (Little and Cantor 1970, p. 127). And acting teachers can be heard to warn their students not to try "to swallow a part whole." Bergler highlights such phrases as "digesting the part" and "the actor's bread and butter." His patient, who saw the house as "an open mouth," also reported that "while studying my part I had the impression that somebody wants to force something down into my throat and I resist violently" (1949, p. 318). Learning lines, for example, is one of the first acts of "taking in" (internalization) that the actor performs and the mode of internalization, that is, the underlying (oral) incorporative fantasies, is attested to by the surprisingly large number of actors who report that this onerous job is usually accomplished while eating a meal. The learning of lines is often resisted precisely because it represents an internalization that signals the start of the phase in rehearsals when the actor will really have to use what's inside him, his own emotions.

Audiences come to the theater to be entertained, but Sybil Thorndike, who had the courage to "look at the audience," understands that entertainment in the theater is always a form of feeding. She gives the following advice to the audience: "In order to appreciate the flavor of Gracie Fields or Edith Evans—I suggest spare feeding, because through these artists, and their like, you will be filled to overflowing with the food of life which will better spread to all parts of your body if it is not clogged with meat, poultry, suet, and ice cream" (1932, p. 302). It was also Dame Sybil who told Olivier that she and her husband, Sir Lewis Casson, take pills to combat their stage fright. This suggests that the direct oral incorporation of the drug—or alcohol, as with Actor B—has given the actor something "good" to swallow to offset whatever is "bad" inside him.

At the same time as the actor wants to be fed, he fears the insatiable hunger of the audience. In an essay on the psychological implications of theater architecture, called "The Primal Cavity," Kaplan (1968) refers to the actor's "experience [of] the audience as a unified, demanding force, entirely free of obligations to think or act—a kind of *thoughtless hunger* emanates from the auditorium . . . *a voracity*" (p. 107; italics added). This "thoughtless hunger" is experienced by the actor as the audience's aggressive demand to be fed.

The fear of "being eaten up" by the audience is also a projection of the actor's own wish to feed off them, to devour the "house." As with most paranoid delusions, there is a kernel of truth. The actor's projected unacceptable instinctual wish for the milk of human kindness is anchored to some genuine detail in the external world and he finds a ready receptacle for his projection in the voyeuristic appetite of the audience. The aggression that is mobilized within the actor toward the audience temporarily turns them into a bad, persecuting "presence" in the "house."

In short, there are active aggressive fields, established on both sides of the proscenium, which merge and reinforce each other during the opening moments of performance.

This aggression almost always carries with it an oral significance.

As we have seen, disturbances of the gastrointestinal tract are among the commonest symptoms of stage fright, for example, vomiting, nausea, diarrhea, and (Stapleton's) belching. In such instances, the content of the actor's fear is being expressed through body language; the anxiety has been somatized. The actor harbors a wish to swallow an audience whose mental image has been contaminated by his own projected aggression. "Dis-gust," in its Latinate root, speaks to the fantasies that underlie such symptoms: the actor must expel the bad presence within him. For an audience not to approve, not to participate in the drama, leaves the actor feeling abused and depressed and disgusted. One hears "they didn't like it" or "they weren't with it" after a performance at the same time as one sees actors moving somewhat slowly to their dressing rooms, registering muted self-disgust. George C. Scott, "the high-class hustler," was so affected by a bad audience that "he react[ed] . . . by losing his temper and by getting drunk" (Gelb 1977, p. 11). Once again, after the initial angry outburst, an oral cure has been found for an oral injury.

Furthermore, in speaking of the audience as a bad "presence" in the mind, one recalls the common theater expression, "There's no such thing as a bad audience; only bad actors." While this phrase is meant to warn the young and inexperienced actor not to displace the blame for a poor performance from himself onto the audience, not to be a bad child, it reveals, by its negation, the unconscious truth of what it presumes to deny: "There are only bad audiences; no bad actors." Of course, actors always take the chance that their performance may never work on a particular night but some are rather well defended against this possibility. Duse, after such an evening, remarked, "I am too sick with digust for so coarse—so vulgar an audience. . . . There's a bitter taste in my mouth" (in Gilder 1926, p. 255). (Some audiences can only produce sour milk.) Duse, apparently, could never be bad; it was always the audience's fault. Norma Desmond, confronted by a young writer's observation that she "used to be big in pictures," replied, "I still am big. It's the pictures that have gotten small" (*Sunset Boulevard*; Wilder, Brackett, and Marsham 1950).

Duse and the imaginary Norma Desmond led very different theatrical lives but both managed to sustain a belief in their own omnipotence, Duse through her successes and a kind of willful determination, Norma Desmond through a reclusive delusion. But all actors, in order to perform well, must somehow believe that it is their job to entertain, to do the feeding, not the other way round. An admission of an overly intense hungry neediness would only destroy the very illusion they are trying to create; audiences are uncannily able to sense when an actor is pandering to them. Modell nicely describes such a situation where "the belief in a state of omnipotent self-sufficiency exists side by side with an intense and overwhelming dependency expressed as a craving hunger for admiration and approval" (1976, p. 302). This is the actor's intrapsychic plight in the moments before performance.

When an actor's faith in his own talent is severely shaken, he may be forced to confront his "craving hunger for admiration and approval." His intense feelings of (oral) dependency and aggression toward the audience are admitted into consciousness and a defeatist, apathetic attitude envelops his work. This is actually another dynamic involved in states of numbness and unnatural calm, discussed in the following paragraph. Even a successful actor like Richard Burton (1976) admitted, with a faint smile, that what he enjoyed about the theater was the applause. But an unsuccessful, beaten actor, like Archie Rice, in John Osborne's *The Entertainer* (1957), creatively dies when he is forced to acknowledge his own hunger. At the final curtain, he bitterly and openly challenges his audience, while admitting that all along, they, and not he, have been the true entertainers: "You've been a good audience. Very good. A very *good* audience. Let me know where you're working tomorrow night—and I'll come and see you" (p. 89).

In certain instances, the death of the creative spark within the actor has been signaled by continuing states of numbness before a performance. Actors accept stage fright as a part of their work to such an extent that they become worried when they feel "nothing" before a performance. Experience has taught them that, under such circumstances, their work will not be very good that night. "Either I suffer or my work suffers; what a business," said Actress E. Margot Fonteyn (1976) recalls that "when the long awaited night was upon me, I became unnaturally calm, which worried Pamela May terribly. 'Are you all right?' she asked. 'You're always so nervous before the performance. I've never seen you like this.' In fact, I was completely numb" (p. 35).

Accompanying states of "numbness," actors often report feelings of fatigue, listlessness, and a loss of appetite as well as thoughts about not wanting to perform that night. While such states may be subsumed under Kaplan's notion of "blocking . . . a total extinction of impulse by disconnecting the self from all avenues of functioning" (1969, p. 64), they are more likely evidence of an underlying depression. Dorpat (1977) makes a crucial distinction between anxiety and depression. "One feels anxiety over something painful that might happen, but one experiences depressive affect about something painful which has happened or that one has some certainty will happen" (p. 5; also see Brenner 1982).

Viewed in this light, the actor's unnatural calm is evidence of having thrown in the towel, as it were, conceding defeat in advance. His predictions of a bad performance are self-fulfilling prophecies. Chronic states of numbness are rarely seen, perhaps because such actors ultimately become unemployable. A high "degree of certainty about the unpleasurable event" is inimical to performing and suggests states of apathy which Bowlby (1973) describes as one of the extreme reactions to intense loss and abandonment. Kaplan "suspect[s] that a person who begins to perform at some point in his life miraculously free of stage fright will sooner or later leave the stage. Complete freedom from stage fright occurs in those with a modicum of talent" (1969, p. 83).

Given the "regressive context" of the work, the acting process is (intrapsychically) dangerous. When we have concluded our investigation, we will be in a better position to understand how and why stage fright is a necessary component of all good acting. Anxiety, and not depression, has a creative solution because depression is in response to a fantasy about a loss that has already occurred. Depression does not admit of probability; anxiety does. Therefore, I am inclined to agree with Kaplan when he speculates that the total absence of stage fright occurs only in those with limited talent.

Certainly, from my own personal experience with very gifted actors over the past twenty-five years, I can say that some degree of anxiety has accompanied their performance work every step of the way. We should only underscore the phrase, "complete freedom," in Kaplan's formulation in order to avoid a gross overgeneralization. As we have already noted, one of the mysteries of stage fright is that sometimes it's there, sometimes it isn't; some nights it is very intense and some nights it's hardly felt at all. I believe this has to do with the fact that actors are able to make use of themselves in different ways on different evenings. The processes involved in the transformation of the personal self into the performing self, that is, the character, are complex and are subject to an infinite number of variables, having to do with the entire state of the actor's psychic life during a particular twenty-four-hour period.

But one thing we can be sure of: actors are courageous people in their willingness to engage in such a profound process of self-examination and self-exposure; acting is a radical procedure. Ingmar Bergman once noted that "Rigor and dizziness are necessary for inspiration. . . . The dangerous routes are finally the only viable ones" (1978). And, David Belasco remarked, "I wouldn't give a nickel for an actor who isn't nervous" (Little and Cantor 1970, p. 93).

5

THE ARTISTIC PROBLEM OF STAGE FRIGHT

The performance is a happening. It is the intrinsically poetic moment; the moment, when, with the spectators' presence contributing the final drop, the chemical precipitate appears. The performance is an act of love: one gives, one gives oneself, exchanges and communes.

—Jean-Louis Barrault

Vanishing Act

No actor that I have ever directed, taught, or interviewed has ever experienced the extreme symptomatology of stage fright without an audience and for a long time I was concentrating on the impact of its arrival as the only catalyst for the traumatic anxiety attack until I recognized that something else happens when the audience arrives and that is, of course, that the director leaves. It also occurred to me that my own resistance to dealing with this simple fact had to do with certain painful feelings that I experienced on opening nights: specifically, conflicts about having been abandoned by *my* actors and having entrusted to *them* certain aspects of my own self-esteem. On opening night, then, we actually have an exquisite irony where both partners to an abruptly severed relationship (including its unconscious, transferential aspects) are experiencing, each in their own way, a sense of loss.

The actor unconsciously experiences the first public performance as an abandonment on the part of the director; it is this unconscious sense of abandonment and loss that ultimately triggers the final phase of the stage fright attack. Suddenly, the director has disappeared or, to put it less theatrically, the director's rehearsal relationship with the actor has been abruptly terminated without its transferential aspects having been dissolved, analyzed, or worked through. The director is no longer seen, heard, or experienced as a protective presence. In his place, literally in the place where he used to sit, we have the audience.

"The mystery man" is how Walter Kerr has described the director. "You can see the actors and you can at least say how they look and what they wore. The playwright is tangible through his words, but *the director has vanished*" (Little and Cantor 1970, p. 246; italics added). The illusion of the play's reality depends upon the invisibility of the director's activities. If the actor's goal is to present a spontaneous and truthful image of the character's behavior, then any intimation of a guiding hand behind the scenes, a director as puppet master, would destroy this illusion.

For instance, at the very end of *Tea and Sympathy*, director Elia Kazan used a follow spot to outline Deborah Kerr during her final speech. The general stage lighting dimmed; suddenly, Kerr's body was illuminated by a sharp circle of light. It seemed that Kazan had intruded himself on the action, drawing attention away from the life of the characters. Sometime later, however, Kazan used two follow spots to great effect in *Sweet Bird of Youth*, but these were introduced at the very start of the production and became part of the rules of the game. They were accepted as a convention. It is, therefore, possible for a director to devise highly theatrical effects and still preserve the illusion of his invisibility. Peter Brook's masterful production of *A Midsummer Night's Dream* is a case in point.

While the director will visit the cast in their dressing rooms before the curtain, offering a smile and a "good luck," he will not see them again until after the play. This is the phenomenon of the leaderless group. The director, the odd man out, is truly the one who remains in limbo for the entire performance. John Van Druten, a playwright and director, said, "When the final dress rehearsal is over, [the director's] job is done, and he spends the opening night impotently watching, like a coach on the side line" (1945, p. 538). This sense of impotence is pervasive among directors. Of the eleven I talked to informally about their experiences on opening night, all shared with me the same sensations of frustration and helplessness.

What is more, unlike the audience, the director is rarely able to gain any direct pleasure out of watching the performance because he cannot see it as an organic whole; he follows it, moment to moment, anticipating lines of dialogue, gestures, pauses, light and sound cues, and so forth. In fact, some directors, standing at the rear of the theater, can be overheard in what amounts to a semi-silent coaching of the actor, the stage manager, and the crew, almost as if the director wished to tell the audience what he had planned. A few directors even feel as if they were speaking directly to the actors:

> Come on, now. You can do it. The sword. Go for the sword!
> Where's that light cue?
> OK. Here we go. Keep it building. Free it up. Breathe! Now: "The play's the thing," lights down, "wherein" bells—yes—yes—"I'll catch," fade it, fade it, "the conscience of the king!" Fade it and [sigh of relief here] intermission.

If the actor's impulse is to escape just prior to his entrance, the director's is to run up on the stage during the performance to fix things. The impulse is often so strong that it can force a director to spend the opening night pacing the street or in a nearby bar. His frustration is that he has lost "touch" with his actors. The director's experience complements that of the actor who yearns to be in "touch" with his character, the play, and, through them, the audience.

The following recurrent dream, reported by a middle-aged actor, reveals the significance of the fearful separation from the director. This actor experiences moderate to severe stage fright before every public performance. He prefaces his report of the dream by describing a sense of mystery about it because it occurs at random intervals in his life. It does not coincide with opening nights, nor does it seem to coordinate with any other regular aspect of the production process. He has this dream about three or four times a year.

> I am in my dressing room, getting ready for the performance. I realize that my costume is not there. I call for the wardrobe mistress; she doesn't answer. I go out into the hall to find her; she must have my clothes. She is nowhere to be seen. I begin to feel uneasy. I start walking down the hall and realize that I am completely alone backstage. Out front, I can hear the audience taking their seats. I wake up from the dream in a panic.

First of all, this dream demonstrates the multidetermined nature of stage fright described in previous chapters. At one level, it represents the exhibitionistic fear of exposure; his shame (I don't want to be seen) demands that the actor be covered. The change from "my costume" to "my clothes" speaks to the underlying fear of nakedness. His associations also reveal that, while trying to find his clothes, he has the fleeting thought that the wardrobe mistress has "not run off with them but has taken them away to be cleaned." The (anal) messing component is present.

Second, and in a more disguised way, the separation anxiety is evident. The wardrobe mistress–mother's disappearance leads to the frightening realization that the actor is "completely alone backstage" while the audience gathers. The actor reports that he must face the audience all alone, representing the rest of the cast, the author, and the director. He then thinks about the single combat between Achilles and Hector that will decide the fate of the Trojan war (the grandiosity of his narcissism).

In associating to the dream as a whole, the actor notices that he feels the same kind of helpless vulnerability toward it as he does in front of an audience. He hopes that I may be able to interpret the dream for him: he is aware that I am now a psychotherapist, someone who can "direct" his dreams for him. Further thoughts lead the actor away from his curiosity about the dream itself to an explanation of why he currently directs more than he acts. As a director, he feels in control of the entire production; he also senses that the "production" to which he refers is a representation of his own mind. But the dream becomes even clearer when he says, "I guess I always wanted to direct every play I've acted in. I mean, I always wanted to be the director and the actor at the same time. It must be so much easier."

To be "director and actor at the same time" would diminish the painful feelings of separation. In fact, this actor's wife is a psychoanalyst; significantly, she is absent from any of his associations. The actor somewhat casually assumed that the equation, wardrobe mistress = director = wife = mother, was "too close to home."

Here Kaplan's notion, that a disruption in the actor's sense of poise is a major factor in stage fright, illuminates the issue of separation anxiety. Poise is based upon the infant's earliest interactions with the mother. Our adult sense of poise derives from unconscious assumptions that we make about support from an average expectable environment. "Collaborative instrumentalities," as Kaplan calls them, develop between mother and child; they adumbrate ways in which the growing youngster will deal with the threat of the loss of reciprocity. For example, the infant's hand-to-mouth explorations begin to function as autonomous tension-relieving mechanisms, while certain postural mannerisms are adopted "to protect oneself from being 'put down,' dropped, as it were, by another person" (1969, p. 68). At the same time he is responding to the fantasied loss of the director, the actor, we recall, must consciously inhibit any "unmeant gestures" and such gestures often include hand-to-mouth comforting as well as personal "postural mannerisms" that the actor has adopted throughout his life. When stage fright is viewed from this perspective, we can begin to see that it is also a response to "the temporary loss of the collaboration with the attentive presence of the mother" (Kaplan 1969, p. 66).[1]

As the actor's coping mechanisms begin to break down when he is trapped in the wings, the full impact of the abandonment by the director is unconsciously registered. This takes place just before his entrance onto the stage where he already fears the encounter with the audience. Resentment at the director for having abandoned him to the bad audience reinforces the actor's anger at the audience for having robbed him of the good director. Since the field between the actor and audience has already been contaminated with the actor's own sadistic oral greediness, this new "sum of excitation" greatly intensifies both the wish for and the feared loss of attentiveness. Will the audience supply for him the "attentive presence" that the director has given? Furthermore, not only has the director left the actor alone to face the audience. His sudden (intrapsychic) disappearance has also left the actor alone to face his own anxiety, which includes a propensity toward a regression which might carry him beyond the stage of a cohesive self (Kohut 1971).

As we have seen, the actor has used the director as a surrogate for parts of his psychic functioning, particularly as a stimulus barrier, but, in a more comprehensive way, as an auxiliary ego. Suddenly, with no opportunity to come to terms with such a loss, the actor is faced with the necessity of reinstituting these mechanisms on his own. But, by now, the momentum of the regression has built to such a level that the ego is at the outer limits of its endurance. By calling stage fright "morbid anxiety," Kaplan implies that the actor is close to a psychotic break, to an irreversible psychopathological state. In fact, Weissman (1969) developed the concept of a temporary, reversible, creative psychosis that all artists must experience.

The actor predictably gains some relief when he is able to remain in contact with an image of the good director. Seldes tried to imagine "McClintick [her director] in the audience every night" (1978, p. 187). A patient in analysis was about to return to the stage after many years. Preparing on her own for a solo performance, she experienced severe stage fright. She was able to diminish it somewhat by imagining that she had had a director, assisting her in the work right from the start (Jay Harris, personal communication). Other actors report that fleeting memories of their director, memories of his compliments, even of his barbed criticisms—in short, of his "presence"—momentarily relieve the pressure of the anxiety.

Fantasies about the good director and the potentially good audience can be conceived of as existing in one compartment of the mind, while fantasies of the bad, abandoning director and the persecuting audience coexist in another compartment. A division in the mind has taken place as a defensive measure the purpose of which is to keep the "bad presences" walled off from the "good" ones. Some actors feel as if they are "operating mechanically before an audience which is also perceived as quite distant" (Kaplan 1969, p. 64). Naturally, the audience, now a "bad presence," is best kept at a distance. The actor's common perception of a moat between stage and house—this is often the orchestra pit—mirrors and expresses this intrapsychic state of affairs in which the ego, as the executive agency of the mind, is attempting to maintain this division in order to keep the bad "presences" from destroying the good ones. The actor also wants to unite the stage and the house as a conscious performance goal and one of the results of such a union would be a synthesis of the divided, warring "presences" within the ego, leading to peace.

Such processes as a division in the mind, more commonly referred to as "a split in the ego" by psychoanalysts, is not in and of itself a sign of pathology. In everyday life our own acts of self-observation require a division "into sets of functions which can best be described as the observing aspect and the experiencing aspect" (Moore and Fine 1968, p. 89). The performing-actor is predisposed by the nature of his craft to maintain a series of such adaptive splits in the mind. Under ordinary circumstances, for example, we have seen that the actor must hide his awareness of the audience not only from them but also from a part of himself, that part which contains the character, as it were, and which we have called the performing ego.

It is now profitable to refer again to the actors who appeared as career criminals in the prison play. Their stage fright was unusually severe: one of its determinants was traced to castration anxiety, intensified by the "guilty misdeeds" they had to perform (i.e., acting out the characters' homosexuality). But another factor contributed to the pitch of the attack, at least as far as Actor E was concerned. "Emergency measures" had to be instituted during final rehearsals: some of the actors were forced to remain in jail as a way of helping them experience the essence of claustrophobia. On opening night, during the peak of his anxiety, Actor E found that he kept looking back angrily at this incident. Later, he was able to remember that his rage was aimed at the director who, because he could arrange such an "outrageous stunt," seemed to be omnipotent. The more powerful the director became, the more helpless the actor felt. A further complication for Actor E was that he begrudgingly admitted his performance had been lacking a sense of truth about "being in jail" so that a part of him approved of the (good) director's emergency measure.

This illustration not only serves to reinforce the premise that the loss of the director (in this case, his omnipotent magic) was the immediate precipitant of the traumatic anxiety. It also demonstrates a conflict peculiar to all actors. Implicit in Actor E's anger was the wish to be free from the director in order to perform well. The actor recognizes the need to preserve his autonomy at all costs. But this wish comes into conflict with an opposing one: rapprochement with the nurturing director. The actor's bind is a revival of an ubiquitous stage in childhood development, what Mahler, Pine, and Bergmann have called "ambitendency" and have described as the need "to be united with, and at the same time separate from" the mother (1975, p. 292). For the actor as well, each alternative carries its own drawbacks: the former, the fear of loss of autonomy, a re-engulfment, and the latter, the fear of the loss of the mother's presence.

Many actors feel uneasy when the director returns to watch subsequent performances precisely because of the dangers involved in reuniting with him. Goffman says, "Trainers tend to evoke for the performer a vivid image of himself that he had repressed, a self-image of someone engaged in the clumsy and embarrassing process of becoming" (1959, p. 158). The actor has to avoid reactivating such self-images not only because they tend to shake his self-confidence in his ability to play the part, but also because they make it harder to hide from the audience the fact that the play has been rehearsed. In terms of the actor's self-confidence, Goffman further notes that "the performer can make himself forget how foolish he once was, but he cannot make the trainer forget" (p. 159). Too vivid a wish to be reunited with the director throws out of balance the adaptive split in the ego which the actor must maintain between the observing ego and the performing ego. During their finest performances, for example, actors tend to feel that the character (the performing ego) has taken over in the sense that it is not the actor who is making things happen; it is the character who reacts spontaneously and truthfully.

If the actor gives in too soon to his reunion fantasies with the director, the integrity of the performing ego may be compromised. The actor unconsciously yearns for the honeymoon of early rehearsals when he had the freedom to do anything. But this seductive (regressive) pull would, if followed, take the actor back to a time in the development of the character when images of the self and of others had not yet been fully organized into a coordinated performing ego. And, if carried to its extreme, a complete reunion with the early-phase, nurturing director would result in the disintegration of the character, the loss of the through-line of action and the ultimate failure of the performance.

Recall Actress E's comment, "Either I suffer, or my work suffers." It was originally cited in the context of the actor's fear of numbness, the calm before curtain time, which almost always results in a poor performance. Now, her comment takes on new meaning; either I suffer the loss of separation or my work suffers the loss of autonomy.

"I want to rehearse again"

Opening night cannot obliterate the actor's memories of the rehearsal process. The traumatic anxiety state actually reactivates wishes, contained within these memories, to escape to the early rehearsal phase in order to be reunited once again with the lost "presence" of the mother-director image in their "love affair with the world." The wish to rehearse again is yet another indicator of the central role that separation anxiety plays in stage fright.

Paul Newman says, "My fantasy [is that] you get a marvelously inventive director, and you cast it the way it ought to be cast, not because you have to cast it a certain way. You get together and you have four incredible weeks of rehearsal and then you shut it down. And no one ever sees it. You never have an audience to come in and see it." Al Pacino comments, "I sometimes wish that there were no opening nights, that you just rehearsed, and people came, and it just happened" (Probst 1975, pp. 54, 30). Of course, directors share this wish. Peter Hall records in his diary that he "spent all morning rehearsing the first scene of *Hamlet*—four hours—and it was a wonderful experience. It's really why I do this job. Not for performances—not for plays—not for money—but for the satisfaction of having a really good rehearsal where the excitement of discovery spreads from actor to actor" (1984, p. 189).

The wish for an eternal, "incredible" collaboration with the early-phase, "marvelously inventive" director is based upon the actor's memory of a time when he actually had the unlimited freedom to play while in the attentive presence of a nonintrusive mother. The actor understandably has a reluctance to leave his rehearsal home and meet the world. Ways in which actors turn their dressing rooms into little "homes" suggest the existence of pleasurable fantasies, created to combat the house full of strangers which they are about to meet. Such fantasies continue to exist even after opening night but in a new form, leading to a series of adaptive, reality-oriented activities that contribute a sense of vitality and freshness to the work. Since each subsequent performance is a new re-creative experience, it offers the actor an opportunity to continue his exploration of the character.

"I learn something new about the character every night of the run." "When we closed [after approximately 1200 performances], I finally figured out how to play that scene." Such comments from the performing-actor are common-place. For instance, after Laurence Olivier had played *Long Day's Journey into Night* for a year and a half, he told an associate that he had finally found out something new and important about James Tyrone. Olivier "discovered" during the performance that Tyrone ties his high leather boots in a knot from behind. With intense delight, Olivier said, "From behind! Isn't that rather wonderful about the man" (Elizabeth Smith, personal communication).

Such exploration can, however, reinforce some actors' sense of the play-still-in-rehearsal to such an extent that the edge is taken off their performances. A serious problem with the Actors Studio training program was that it did not make a sufficient distinction between rehearsal and performance technique. The mumbling, inarticulate, painfully slow pace of many performances in the fifties and sixties was a result not only of bad acting technique but also of a refusal to acknowledge the reality-oriented fact that performances make new, stringent demands on the actor *to communicate with the outside world, with the audience.*

A further examination of the events at a final dress rehearsal of *Hamlet*, outlined earlier, can help deepen our understanding of how this wish "to rehearse again" functions. Actor B stopped the work because he had "lost the pitch of the house." Stopping the dress was, in part, a manifestation of Actor B's wish to continue rehearsing, to reestablish contact with his director and the emotionally laden sentence was "Can you [i.e., his director] help me find it?" But the actor's behavior, following his request, demonstrated that he did not need the director's "help" at all. Actor B, on his own, found "the pitch"; the director obviously could not perform this complicated act of sensory-motor (vocal) coordination for the actor.

His director, G, later said that, while making "a big show" of sending assistants off to check air conditioners and exit doors, he winked at his associates to let them know that they need not act out this charade. (Actor B could not see this; the director was in the balcony.) G had worked with this actor before: "He's always doing something like that. He just can't seem to let go. And, besides, we were doing the show in the middle of winter. What air conditioners?"

It is also useful to mark the precise moment in the scene when Actor B stopped the rehearsal. It was just before Hamlet's first soliloquy; all the other actors exit, leaving Actor B alone on stage. It would seem, then, that the actor's need to stop was also a way of handling his separation anxiety, an attempt to make contact with the lost, or to be more precise, the being lost intrapsychic "presence" of the director. A soliloquy, of course, brings the actor face to face with the (bad) audience, intensifying the dread of exposure, retaliation, and isolation. Olivier, as Othello, asked his Iago to stand by him during his soliloquies. But this Hamlet did not make the same request of his Horatio because he was the kind of person who could not admit to any weakness in himself and this would have been the case had he acknowledged his personal vulnerability to stage fright.[2]

Strictly speaking, this example is not one of stage fright. The tension Actor B experienced instituted an adaptation to the environment. Actor B's "signal" did not ignite the powder keg; his anxiety did not proceed to a traumatic state. Because he was not actually trapped in performance conditions, he still had access to poise-restoring mechanisms. But the defense used was quite primitive: a denial of the rules of the dress-rehearsal game. It is extremely rare to find an actor stopping the work at this stage of the production process.

A final, biographical note about this actor: B's dress rehearsal performance was brilliant. But his opening night was, to say the least, disappointing. The public might have seen one of the definitive performances of Hamlet had it not been for his inability to solve the problem of stage fright. It was not possible to determine why the gin, which became a part of Actor B's performing life, affected him in such a destructive way on that particular opening night. B still manages to perform excellently, though he now appears more often in films. When B acts on stage, he wears a hearing aid, which is, in fact, a receiver. It is in contact with the stage manager who, through a cordless transmitter, feeds B almost every line he must say a split second before the cue. Actor B can no longer remember his words.

"This nightmare/daymare . . ."

Of all the phrases Actor B could have chosen to find the pitch of the house, he spontaneously hit upon "to be," which he repeated numerous times. This free association, as it were, then served the actor to reaffirm his sense of self (at least in its observing aspect) in the face of the potential loss of the director, less than twenty-four hours away.

"To be or not to be" leads to the last and most significant determinant of stage fright. If the catalyst for the traumatic anxiety attack is the actor's inability to cope with the abandonment by the director, then at its core is a fear of the loss of the sense of self. While others (mainly Gabbard 1979, 1983 and Kaplan 1969) have ably demonstrated how regressively revived fears of the anticipated loss of collaboration with mother are among the most significant genetic determinants of stage fright, my focus has been on the more immediate lost "presence," both interpersonal and intrapsychic, of the director. His "vanishing act" has specific impact on the immediate work task that confronts the performing-actor.

Throughout rehearsals, the director has functioned as the actor's observing ego, and, even though in the final rehearsal phase, the actor attempts to reinternalize this function through an identification with the director, the pressures of opening night tend to undo such a process. The loss of the "presence" of the director is registered unconsciously as a loss of the observing ego.

"There is no place for objectivity in rehearsal. The director must be the sole possessor of that attribute while the play is being discovered" (Seldes 1978, p. 204). Having ceded over to the director one's self-observing, self-critical functions time and time again, in play after play, it is very difficult for the actor to reclaim them on opening night. It is not uncommon to find actors inquiring about the worth of their performance after having played the part for over a year. These questions are not in the service of an insatiable or coy narcissism, nor are they game playing. The actor simply can never be sure of how his performance actually looks from out front. Katharine Hepburn is credited with the observation that she finally felt secure as an actress, rather late in her career, when she did not have to read the opening night notices anymore.

Actors often get so deeply involved in their roles that it takes them time to return to reality after a performance. Richard Burbage, Shakespeare's leading actor, is said to have taken about two hours to "get out of" playing Richard III. Basil Rathbone may have stopped playing Sherlock Holmes partly because he felt in danger of becoming controlled by Doyle's character. During one curtain call of Stoppard's *The Real Thing*, Jeremy Irons was so enmeshed in the character that he stood, somewhat glazed, singing the song with which he ended the play as if the action were still continuing.

The clearest statement of this theme in film is *Dead of Night*, in which the ventriloquist (Michael Redgrave) ultimately becomes the puppet-slave to his "dummy." A less successful but more extended treatment of the same process, occurs in the film, *A Double Life*, in which an actor's portrayal of Othello invades his personal life, leading him to murder his Desdemona-slut. *Six Characters in Search of an Author* can be seen as another artistic representation of this state of affairs. The "characters," who interrupt the rehearsal, stand for the actors' performing egos, while the director, who wants to get on with the business of rehearsing a new comedy, represents the observing ego. As the play reaches its climax, the performing egos take over and their incestuous and violent drama is finally played out. The repressed has banished the repressing defenses from the stage, culminating in a creative psychosis, a total dissolution of the observing ego into its performing counterpart.

The actor, trapped in the wings, cannot remove himself from his fantasy, that is, from the character he is creating/re-creating; "the show must go on" and so the performing ego must be protected at all costs. The observing ego acts as a buffer and a link to reality for the performing ego but, robbed of the observing ego–director, and as yet not having made contact with the stabilizing, holding environment of an attentive audience, the threat is that the character might gain complete access to motility and the actor would be left with what amounts to a false self. Kaplan recognizes such a threat when he speaks of "a final dissolution of the personal self [i.e., observing ego] into performance" (1969, p. 70); Gabbard refers to stage fright as "disintegration anxiety" (1983, p. 431). Actors also recognize this threat by indirection: a favorite trick among some is to carry with them a small personal possession in the pocket of their costume as a sort of "rabbit's foot," a good-luck charm. This concrete object, to which the actor can refer, also helps him get back in touch with his "personal self" should its regressive dissolution become too imminent.

Florence Eldridge referred to performing as "a schizophrenic experience." She was using the term in its colloquial sense, with the accent on the "split" she feels when acting. Others have noted the same phenomenon within themselves, but none have described it as well as Marian Seldes:

> Your part becomes your life and if it is—if you are— threatened, your behavior becomes extreme to anyone not connected with the play. It is what the analysts might call schizophrenia, which we are told is "a psychosis marked by withdrawn sometimes delusional behavior and by intellectual and emotional deterioration." This delusion, this conception that resists reason and logic and matters of actual fact, is often the state the actor finds himself in not only at rehearsals but in performance. He is separated: He is himself. He is the part. He is the child who learned the part and he is the artist playing the part. He can do no wrong. He can fail miserably. He lives in this nightmare/daymare throughout his working life. It is how he controls his "schizophrenia" that sets him apart from the indulgent amateur or the inspired nut. [1978, p. 95]

Since the (internalized) director's anticipated loss can be seen as a loss of that part of the ego that has access to the actor's own identity, then a reunion with the director's "presence," on stage during performance, restores the actor's sense of wholeness. *The medium through which this reintegration takes place is the audience.* The good director image has been merged with that of the good audience and these good "presences" have been kept alive in one compartment of the mind. The audience is a very concrete representation of an observing ego (and judgmental superego) and the attention it finally pays to the actor restores his sense of wholeness. Glen Gabbard accurately highlights this aspect when he says that stage fright is not *self-*consciousness "but *other-*consciousness, i.e., *audience-*consciousness" (1983, p. 439).

Sybil Thorndike refers to "that curious sensation we have when entering the stage, as of *one's other half-being waiting*" (1932, p. 301; italics added). And Seldes asks, "Who is the audience? What does it mean to the actor? Is it what it looks like: a group of people? Or is it one person the actor invents and puts there to watch: a part of himself that is neither the actor nor the character but what the great Italian actor Salvini called 'a third self'?" (1978, p. 186).

These actresses are describing, in metaphor, intrapsychic processes. In both quotations the audience is viewed as an entity which seems to complete something, to fill an empty space within the actor. A commonplace in the psychoanalytic consultation room is the way in which the therapist sometimes has to function as the patient's observing ego during periods of great stress; the therapist must temporarily substitute for a deficient aspect of the patient's psychic functioning. Seldes's notion that the audience is an invented part of the actor, "put there to watch," suggests that the combined audience-director image comes to represent that particular aspect of the actor's psychic functioning that he recognizes may be deficient, namely, his observing ego.

In his essay "On Acting," one of the few on this subject in the psychoanalytic literature, Otto Fenichel spoke about "the double-edged character" of play (1946, p. 355). On the one hand, it is "an anti-surprise measure . . . [it] provides for the actor a belated getting-rid of anxieties, or a defensive anticipation of possible future anxieties" (1946, p. 353). But the pleasure of this kind of play can turn into displeasure when it threatens to become "real," when the actor might become his part forever. The ancestry of the actor's play can be found in child's play where a similar threat exists. In the case of children, however, one is more accustomed to this state of affairs because the boundaries between *in here* and *out there*, between fantasy and reality, are still in the process of being reinforced. In adults, the fluidity of such boundaries, the de-differentiation of self and other images can signal the onset of a psychotic break. "If the child playing 'Mommy' really becomes 'Mommy,' that would be too anxiety provoking. The moment of *transition* is the point where the anxiety breaks in, the ego at that moment feeling threatened by dissolution. It *cannot* remove itself from fantasy" (Lissa Weinstein, personal communication).

So, too, with the actor: it is at "the moment of *transition*" between his personal self and the fully lived being of the character in front of an audience that stage fright breaks in. In some way, the actor must recapture his observing ego in order to let his character breathe; he can only do this with the reassurance that, after all, it's only a play. Therefore, contact with the audience, which includes reunion with the director, restores the actor's sense of wholeness. There is no such thing as a complete performance without an audience because there is no such thing as a complete actor capable of sustaining an adaptive split between his observing and performing ego without the holding "presence" of the audience. Paraphrasing Yeats, one might summarize the actor's basic dilemma: How can we know the actor from the act?

Contact

One of the most intriguing aspects of stage fright is that it can disappear even in the face of a negative response. In other words, it is not solely approval that reverses the attack. It is the audience's acknowledgment, in whatever form it takes, of *the presence of the actor*. While it is true that actors unconsciously fear their phallic exhibitionism, their angry demands for a loving approval of what they have produced, and their sadistically tinged hunger, the fact that stage fright remits in the face of any response from the audience is of great significance. The opposite of love is not hate, but indifference and, while love and hate are predicated on the existence of a relationship with a significant other, indifference reinforces the sense of isolation. No one may be out there; no emotionally receptive or responsive "presence" may be in the house. This lack of a mirroring presence anticipates and sometimes confirms the loss of the sense of self. Kaplan has already noted that the actor's deepest fears are "fashioned out of a real and truly momentous possibility: *the audience's indifference* to the performance" (1969, p. 64; italics added).

One extreme and rather amusing example of a negative response was furnished by an elderly performer. Actress F, playing the part of Nina in *The Seagull*, found her stage fright vanished when she asked Trigorin, the famed writer, "Should I become an actress?" Before the actor could reply, the entire audience exclaimed, "No!" Actress F was nearing seventy; Nina is twenty. Real threats are easier to deal with than fantasied ones.

Of course, the actor hopes for and often receives a significantly positive response: overt laughter and applause or that stunning silence (the pin-drop one). These are the moments when the actor has captured the imagination of the entire audience; when, in fact, he has welded those thousand different strangers into one solid looking-listening-responding unit; when he has created for himself the grandest gleaming eye in the world—an audience. At that precise moment, the stage fright completely disappears and in its place: an experience of elation, of omnipotence—a feeling that the actor can do anything.

Frequently, actors will perform in front of an audience made up largely of members of the profession, either at an Actors' Fund benefit or at "gypsy run-throughs," in which colleagues attend to help the actor get a feel for the play in the house. These performances are usually of great pleasure for the actor and seem to generate much less stage fright. The actor's "presence" is never in doubt, nor is this audience ever truly indifferent.

Such audiences are not strangers to the craft; their ability to understand the technical aspects of the work and to appreciate nuances of an actor's performance create an immediate field of reciprocity. My findings in this regard differ from Glen Gabbard, who notes that "an audience of peers seems to arouse the most stage fright." He says that "performers tend to be an envious lot" and are therefore incapable of watching another's work without to some extent putting it down (1983, pp. 433 ff.). In other words, the actor on stage assumes the same degree of envy in the audience as he himself experiences when seeing a play. Gabbard refers to a twenty-five-year-old actor who kept thinking to himself, "I can play that role ten times better than he can. Why don't they give me a chance?" This actor stopped going to plays for a while because he could not cope with such narcissistic mortification.

I suspect that the difference in our findings in this respect relates to the fact that my observations and interviews were conducted with a very specific and limited population within the theater community, namely, gifted actors who had achieved prominence and reward in the field. The reader will recall that the question that initiated this investigation was why stage fright is experienced to such an extent by the most distinguished members of the acting profession, its stars. These actors may well comprise the category of those "envied by" Gabbard's twenty-five-year-old, but they themselves may be immune to such feelings because of their privileged position in the profession. Certainly when these actors talk about others, there is a remarkable sense of community and respect.

My findings may also be skewed along another axis. The British actors I interviewed tended to be more forthcoming in their praise and appreciation of another's work than their American counterparts, especially when it came to Shakespeare. In the British theater, there is a distinct sense of tradition being continually enriched by subsequent performances of the same play. Many years ago, for instance, Gielgud was asked whether he had any interest in playing Macbeth; his answer, without any hint of false modesty, was "No." He felt that Olivier had given the definitive performance of that part and that he, Gielgud, preferred to spend what time he had left in the theater exploring other characters in Shakespeare where he might be able to make some new contribution.

But American actors are capable of great appreciation of a colleague's work. This was brought home to me during the final preview of *Father's Day*, where the audience was populated primarily by actors. During a section of the play when Marian Seldes was getting many large laughs, a famous American actor, seated next to me, began talking to himself, in much the same way directors do on opening night. Seldes delivered a punch line which "brought the house down." At that moment, the actor, unable to control his admiration of her technique, grabbed hold of my arm and said, "Watch her! Watch her! She's going for another!" And he was right. Timing the audience's response carefully, Seldes subtly delivered yet another line which miraculously provoked even more laughter and a round of applause for the sheer virtuosity of the work. The theater family was showing its appreciation for an actress's fine technique.

The audience remains the bad presence in the house— the uninvited —threatening to persecute the actor by humiliation, ridicule, starvation, and indifference until the actor has made contact with them, until the stage and house are merged. Actors speak in metaphors having to do with contact, connection, and rapport. There is also a distinct sense of communion in, for instance, Colleen Dewhurst's feeling that "when it's going right, the audience breathes with you" (Mitgang 1983, p. C15).

A sense of merger is also hinted at when Rae Allen says, "You communicate *with*, not *to* an audience" (Little and Cantor 1970, p. 94). But Angela Lansbury is more explicit about a merger of stage and house when she says, "There must come a moment when there's nothing between you [the audience] and what is happening on stage, when you are transported out of yourself. I know by the attention, the quiet, this crackling something that passes between what's going on onstage and what's happening in the audience. It's the moment when [they] allow themselves to come with you" (Probst 1975, p. 233). In another interview, this same actress described the reverse experience, the one of separation in which "the house" has not become "a home." "When I'm on stage, I often think, 'What the hell am I doing here?' I realize that I want to go home" (Ross and Ross 1962, p. 364).

Actors will also describe the "performance high" with phrases like "power," "control," and "waves of love." Richard Burton said, "The minute I walked out on stage in front of an audience, I knew I still had the authority, *the presence*, whatever, and I breathed a secret sigh" (1976, p. 10; italics added). And Tennessee Williams understood it, too. He spoke about those "waves of love coming across the footlights and enveloping the actor. The adulation of a live audience is the only food that feeds [the actor's] deprived ego" (Socarides, cited in Little and Cantor 1970, p. 285). A famous actress put it this way: "To have a thousand people waiting on you for every move. To get to that climactic point when you can hear a pin drop. And it's you they're watching. You're ruling the roost" (Little and Cantor 1970, p. 89). This actress is putting into words the very common experience of a young child, who basks in the loving attentiveness of his parents, an attentiveness that Freud once described as giving the child the feeling of being "the centre and core of creation—'His Majesty the Baby'" (1914, p. 91).

Achieving this contact, however, is not only a precondition for the remission of stage fright; more important, it is the sina qua non of good acting. Otis Skinner suggests: "To my mind a performance is perfect only when the player is keyed to great and resilient elation, when his heart is beating a little faster, when the emotions of his character expose themselves clearly to his eye and color his movement. In that clarity new things born of the moment's impulse suggest themselves" (1938, p. 284). But Otis Skinner also knew that "the audience is the unconscious barometer by which the actor judges the even running of his machine" (p. 281).

Earlier, of course, the actor's conscious barometer has been the director. Skinner is even more explicit in highlighting the merger of the good director and the good audience "presences" when he acknowledges "the wise stage direction of my audience" (p. 282). With regard to her performance in *Father's Day*, Marian Seldes insisted that it was the audience who directed her, who helped her find that extra laugh at the final preview. During dress rehearsals, where the director is most clearly acting as audience, he can remain a "good presence" because he differs from the actual opening night crowd in several crucial respects: he is no stranger, and he does not watch these rehearsals with the same unconscious "thoughtless hunger" as an audience does at a performance.

Contact reverses the traumatic anxiety attack by merging stage and house and releases the actor from his isolation. An emotionally authentic relationship, now characterized by reciprocity and attentiveness, has finally been established. It offers both audience and actor intense gratification. The question of who is feeding whom becomes irrelevant.[3] The polarities of "oneness" and "separateness," which have trapped the actor in an ambivalent, "ambitendent" bind, collapse into a sense of wholeness in which the actor can without fear experience his autonomy in the collaborative presence of significant others. The state of elation, accompanied by feelings of warmth, admiration, affection, and respect, recall Burgess Meredith's exclamation, "There's so much love around, you can't stand it!"

Nevertheless, it is very difficult to get beneath the actor's grandiose omnipotence in order to tease out the implications of this elated state. Actors resist, and rightfully so, being interviewed directly after a performance. For example, Little and Cantor (1970) quote a star as saying, "When you feel you have them, when you know you've got them, what a wonderful feeling" (p. 89). But this suggests the question, "Have them where?" The answers to such questions seem to contain fantasies that relate to the actor's initial subjective experience of stage fright. Actor Q, whose primary coping fantasy was of an anal assault on the audience, felt he had them "by the balls," whereas the actress, whose fear manifested itself more directly in terms of separation, felt she had them "inside my body." Her response was not directly sexual; she was talking about a merger phenomenon, a sense of being filled up and at one with the audience.

Undoubtedly, the shift from passive, helpless vulnerability to active mastery in itself contributes to this elated state. Once the "craving hunger" is satisfied, then an "omnipotent self-sufficiency," which has existed side by side with the hunger and has been contaminated by it, can be fully experienced. At the moment that stage fright stops, some actors feel as if an electric current had passed through their entire bodies, especially to the extremities and the shoulders. This "current" of strength and self-sufficiency accompanies the elated state; it is a pleasurable sensation. But the "current" to which the actor refers also expresses and describes an inner sense of relaxation which permits the "character" to inhabit the actor. The imaginative impulse must move throughout the entire body, "to the tips of the toes, the fingers—all over." This is one of the reasons that actors have been trained extensively in voice production, speech (diction), movement, dance, acrobatics, and some form of physical relaxation and realignment (e.g., the Alexander technique). The body must become a ready receptacle for the imagination. As Michel Saint-Denis once remarked, "Imagination without technique is a form of impudence."

The actor's elation at the departure of stage fright is also in response to the fact that new energies are suddenly at his disposal. Large amounts of psychic energy were devoted to maintaining the defensive split in the ego between the bad "presences" and the good ones. When, however, this splitting mechanism is no longer needed, the energies devoted to it can be displaced onto those activities which insure the integrity of both the observing and the performing ego, in particular, the ability to remain inside the character and outside at the same time. Following Kris (1952), the energy needed to seal off the bad from the good "presences" can be withdrawn and "added to [the] speed, force or intensity with which the preconscious thoughts are formed" (p. 313). Preconscious mental processes have access both to the unconscious and the conscious, that is to say, to repressed wishes and to reality-oriented thinking, to the most primitive and concrete and to the most logical and abstract modes of ideation. During a successful performance, when an actor feels that the character is playing itself, he is describing just such preconscious mental activity.

Negative Capability

Stage fright in the performing actor is ultimately a fear of psychic annihilation. Triggered by the abandonment of the director, who has come to represent the actor's observing ego, stage fright anticipates the dissolution of the personal self into its performing counterpart. This conflict is displaced onto the audience, whom the actor hopes will acknowledge his presence and become a holding environment for his personal self while the actor can give free reign to his performing self.

The actor fears indifference from the audience more than anything else. Love and hate presuppose the existence of a relationship with others; indifference does not. Stage fright has its ancestry in one of the earliest developmental conflicts of life: the infant's progression through separation and individuation from the mother. The actor's first and major rehearsal relationship is to an early-phase director who supplies "good enough mothering" and who is rarely, if ever, indifferent. Even those directors who are disliked and intensely feared offer the actor a relationship that acknowledges the actor's presence. Geraldine Page once said about her experience with John Dexter on *Black Comedy* that she hated every minute of it but would work with him again "at the drop of a hat."

That there is a recapitulation of an early developmental

task can be seen by comparing what we have learned about the psychological birth of a character with the toddler-mother relationship. Louise Kaplan in *Oneness and Separateness: From Infant to Individual* (1978) describes what happens between a mother and her child in terms that could just as well apply to the actor-director bond in the early phases of rehearsal.

> In his exhilarated certainty, the toddler is relatively unaware of the actual presence of his mother in the flesh. He behaves as though her presence were everywhere. Bodily sensations of mastery combine with a magical feeling of oneness with the world to produce the joyous elation of the love affair with the world. . . . Now that he's upright he stands alone center stage. His mother has been relegated to the role of a protective stagehand, ready to catch the toddler if he goes too near the edge, moving props from here to there so he won't hurt himself, standing by to service his needs. Like an acrobat's assistant, she waits in the wings, attentively watching and listening as the skillful manipulator of space performs his daring balancing acts. [Pp. 167–68]

Later, during final rehearsals, the actor and director seem to recapitulate the beginnings of what Margaret Mahler has called the rapprochement phase of the separation-individuation process; once again, Louise Kaplan's language captures its essence.

> Just recently, the toddler's entire emotional investment was in activity for activity's sake. He couldn't have cared less about who noticed him or watched him or shared with him [the early-rehearsal phase: to play out the objective]. Now the world and its treasures are meaningful when he can share them with another person—above all with his mother. Each time his mother joins him or responds positively to his wooing gestures the toddler staves off the full realization that *he is alone in the world as a separate person who is expected to stand on his own two feet and do everything on his own.* [P. 188; italics added]

Still later, as we have seen, the actor, like the child, is caught in the center of the rapproachement crisis: "He tries to coerce his mother into being one with him. If she gives in to his coercion, he dreads the loss of his selfhood. If she resists and doesn't act as though she and he are part of each other, he comes face to face with his aloneness in the world. Even minor frustrations awaken the longing for oneness and also the dread of oneness" (L. Kaplan 1978, p. 193). Compare this with Peter Hall's description (1984) of the final rehearsal phase of *Happy Days* with Peggy Ashcroft:

> Peg was very obstinate, resisting everything, arguing. She was like a horse who wanted to go, and I wouldn't let her. It is the usual tension with her in the last stages of rehearsal. She wants no detailed work, only to run. And if things are not working she finds it impossible to run. . . . [At a note session] Peggy's eyes were full of tears. She could take no more. This, I've always suspected, is a weapon she is inclined to use unconsciously in the last stage of rehearsal to get the director off her back, though her distress is real. [Pp. 131–32]

This is the domain of stage fright. Peggy Ashcroft's tears sent a message to her director "to get off her back," a message that he apparently received. But the tears presumably signaled the inner conflict surrounding separation-individuation from the director and the feared loss of the autonomous, personal self.

I have used "personal self" throughout, rather than "real self," to avoid semantic difficulties with the word "real," whose implicit opposite is "false." In no way does the actor experience his performing self as "false." In fact, it may sometimes feel as authentic as his personal self (see Weissman 1969, pp. 114–16). Along these lines, the late Gilbert Voyat (personal communication) wondered whether the actor's sense of authenticity and aliveness does not actually reside in his performing self, while the personal self may feel less immediate and more vulnerable. He implied that some actors may have a psychotic core to their character structure around which the performing self has been erected as a defense. Voyat's formulation, by the way, still preserves the psychodynamic (conflictual) basis of stage fright. At the same time, it recalls Winnicott's observation (1952) that

There is a state of affairs in which the fear is of a madness, that is to say a fear of a *lack of anxiety at regression* to an unintegrated state [i.e., the fragmented self], to absence of a sense of living in the body. . . . The fear is that there will be no anxiety, that is to say, that there will be a regression, from which there may be no return. The consequence of this is a repeated testing of capacity for anxiety and temporary relief whenever anxiety is felt, the worse the better. [P. 100]

This suggests yet another reason that some actors submit themselves to stage fright night after night; they do so as a form of prophylaxis.

The intense and transference-laden relationship with the director sets the stage for the fear of the loss of self, the collapse of the observing ego. This study has attempted to demonstrate ways in which such a relationship is established, nurtured, abruptly terminated, and finally recaptured. But outside the realm of the theater a similar process may also occur. As Heinz Kohut speculated, "certain creative personalities appear to require a specific relationship . . . during periods of intense creativity" (1971, p. 316). Kohut had in mind the bonds that existed between Freud and Fliess, James Joyce and James Stephens, Picasso and Braque, and Melville and Hawthorne. He continued:

This need is especially strong when the discoveries lead the creative mind into lonely areas that had not previously been explored by others. The sense of isolation of the creative mind is both exhilarating and frightening, the latter because *the experience repeats traumatically an early childhood fear of being alone, abandoned, unsupported*. In such a situation even the genius may choose a person in his environment whom he can see as all-powerful, as a figure with whom he can temporarily blend. [P. 316; italics added]

Stage fright is not something to be gotten rid of. It is a separate artistic problem which the actor must solve "along with other problems of artistic performance" (D. Kaplan 1969, p. 60).[4] Furthermore, Glen Gabbard, approaching the issue slightly differently, knows that something special would be lost in a theatrical performance were the actor not to experience stage fright. He understands that it "adds a unique dimension to the vitality of live performance. It is emblematic of *the electric interaction* between the performer and the audience that makes the theater a place of magic. . . . As the performer balances on the razor's edge of the audience's ambivalent empathy for him, a sense of dangerous excitement is created" (1983, p. 440; italics added).

The chief artistic problem that an actor faces is how to build a character, how to transform himself so fully into the life of another that on stage he actually believes in his character's life and can effortlessly behave like that person. The more gifted the actor, the greater the degree of transformation. But transformation is not simply imitation. The actor's work includes the imitation of certain behavioral traits in others, but such imitation must be fuelled by imaginative and emotional resources deeply embedded within the actor's own personality. The gifted actor can be defined as one who has the capacity to make use of himself in the most personal way while, at the same time, never losing touch with the more formal demands of the text. In other words, he can turn his private dreams into public realities.

Stage fright intervenes in that gap between the actor as person and the actor as performer. Regardless of individual differences, each actor must make the journey night after night from an everyday self into a performing self and this almost always entails a journey through fear. But we need no longer be surprised that stage fright does not go away, that in some cases it gets worse, and that its intensity varies in a random fashion. After all, no actor is able to bring the full force of his personality to bear on every role he plays nor can he do so during every performance he gives of the same part. The degree of personalization and imaginative reconstruction in creating a role will vary greatly.

At this point in my own understanding of the acting process, I am struck by the intensity of both the interpersonal and the intrapsychic pressures that affect the actor in his working life. The crucial difference between the actor and other performing artists is that he attempts to become someone else—become, not impersonate. Musicians, dancers, and opera singers experience performance nerves but only the actor is forced to experience the primal anxiety of self-transformation. The massive and sudden shifts of psychic energy that take place within the ego as images of the self and of others are coordinated into a performing self do not, in general, lead to permanent pathological states of near dissolution. Such shifts in the actor's narcissistic "balance sheet" (Sandler and Rosenblatt 1962, p. 143) are reversible. The actor is able to sustain a state of being "in uncertainties, Mysteries, doubts, without any irritable reaching after fact and reason," that state which Keats called "Negative Capability."

In short, I am struck by the resiliency of the actor to pressures that in others might lead to psychotic episodes. Perhaps the actor is able to control his "nightmare/day-mare" precisely because he permits himself to experience stage fright. Indeed, we may discover that Winnicott is right, that actors are people who have to expose themselves to anxiety in order to maintain their saneness. The actor, pretending to be Julius Caesar, feels traumatic anxiety while the delusional schizophrenic, believing himself to be Caesar, does not. The actor is able to encompass the worlds of reality and fantasy by bringing them together through the medium of his performance and his capacity to return to reality may lie in his ability to solve the artistic problem of stage fright.

NOTES

Chapter 1

1. Shakespeare carefully and shrewdly introduced phrases and sentences into his text that helped create the mise en scène for his audience: "But look, the morn in russet mantle clad / Walks o'er the dew of yon high eastward hill" (*Hamlet*, I.i.166). If his poetry is given a chance to work, it can have far greater reverberations than even the most accurate, photo-realistic "morn" supplied by the set and lighting designers.

Peter Brook said, without bravado, "I can take an empty space and call it a bare stage. A man walks across this empty space whilst someone else is watching him, and this is all that is needed for an act of theatre to be engaged" (1968, p. 9). Brook's own production of *The Tragedy of Carmen* beautifully demonstrated that he meant what he said. Since Wilder's *Our Town*, there has been an increasing number of noteworthy plays, conceived to be performed without many of these secondary tools, which place virtually all the emphasis on the actor. I am thinking here of *Waiting for Godot* as a prime example of this new, nonrepresentational genre in the twentieth century. It has also been explored in the work of such directors as Grotowski (1968) and Serban (Blumenthal 1977).

2. I am indebted to my colleague Michael Kahn for helping me to conceptualize the complex process of acting in this way.

3. It is almost as if the actor treats the text of the play as the manifest content of a dream. What has come to be known as the "subtext" is somewhat similar to Freud's method for the interpretation of a dream. Essentially, having divided up the script into actable "units," the actor tries to fill in its gaps by creating from his

own imagination the text's deep structure, its subtext. This method often resembles free association.

Chapter 2

1. Staging a play was never a problem. Center stage was usually held by the character with the highest rank, often the king. The others stood on either side of him in descending order governed by the sociopolitical hierarchy.

2. This is the way in which Menninger describes the implicit contract between the patient and the therapist at the start of treatment (1958, pp. 15–76).

3. The objective, I want to get help from the director, is really a new edition of an earlier one: I want to get the part from the director. "The part," which the director possesses, and the action of getting it promote unconscious fantasy elaboration. In the process of casting, an all-powerful authority figure chooses his children to play games. The actor has been selected from a group of invisible rivals; he has become one of the chosen few. Moreover, casting is a very mysterious business. Actors are never quite sure why they have been chosen. No one is able to tell them in any meaningful way what characteristics, what qualities the director is looking for. The mystery is increased by the anonymity of their competitors.

Because the actor can find no rational explanation for why he has been chosen, his imagination is free to construct all sorts of fantasies to explain his victory. Even when an actor does not get the part, his tendency is to blame himself or his invisible competitors: "I gave a lousy reading" or "I wasn't right for the part." Rarely does he blame the director. In other words, the actor's reality-testing regarding the director is momentarily impaired.

4. As bits and pieces of clothing were added, they took on the same quality of fetishistic objects and consequently revived in each actor some measure of repressed castration anxiety. (The actors' dream-lives spoke eloquently enough to this last point.)

5. For purposes of analysis, it is convenient to divide the rehearsal process into three phases: the opening, the middle, and the final phase. These phases overlap; nowhere are their boundaries as clearly defined as they will seem to appear in what follows.

6. When actors talk about a scene, this may promote too much intellectualization so that it is sometimes necessary to eliminate temporarily this route of discharge of instinctual pressure. Although great tension can be experienced, it does help to start an

"adaptive regression in the service of the ego" (Bellack, Hurvich, and Gediman 1973).

7. Often a "no" is rephrased so that its prohibitive tone is transformed into a collaborative affirmation. Director D has disciplined himself to avoid the use of the word "no" throughout all of his rehearsals.

8. Most directors seem to avoid direct interpretations of aggression and sexuality. If they are necessary, they are best left until later in the work. They are useless earlier because the actor would not know what to do with them. They are dangerous because the actor might be impelled to erect strong defenses against their emergence. But there is an even more persuasive reason for withholding such observations: the actor may well come upon such things himself. The optimal situation is when the actor makes his own discoveries about the character. Such insights give the actor a sense of authenticity and autonomy in a way in which no interpretation offered by the director can. Of course, the actor's sense of authenticity about what he is doing plays an important part in the stage fright attack.

This example, by the way, also illustrates the necessity of transforming all the verbal cues of the text into actable terms. "Her eyes go blind with tenderness" is something the actress must try to ignore. It is not playable; it is not doable. Some actors cross out all stage directions in their scripts before the first rehearsal. In fact, Director C always presented his casts with specially prepared scripts which had no stage directions typed in except for "enter" and "exit." Of course, Shakespeare's scripts had almost no descriptive stage directions in them either, only instructions for entrances and exits. Many contemporary actors feel a bit uneasy about this until they learn that Shakespeare embedded his "directions" within the text, within the dynamics of his verse.

9. Another way of looking at the actor's preparation is as a form of behavior modification, rehearsals as a regime of reinforcement of certain stimuli and responses. It is beyond the scope of this study to carry forth such an inquiry.

10. Actors, at this stage of the work, experience what poets do when they describe how the poem wrote itself. For an excellent investigation of this aspect of creativity, see Burnshaw 1970. B. F. Skinner (1972) argues that "a poet can no more take credit for a poem he wrote than a goose can for the golden egg it lays" (p. 32).

11. Disgust is a particularly meaningful response. It suggests a regression to the oral stage of development with potential fantasies of incorporation of the director. The disgust is a compromise formation between the wish to devour and the defense against it.

12. "Transference" will be used because it seems less ponderous and more economical than "transference reactions" or "transference phenomenon." But I agree with Greenson (1967) that "transference reactions" is a more accurate term, since it implies the ebb and flow of such phenomena.

13. Imitation can have its adaptive as well as defensive aspects: the latter seen most clearly, perhaps, in identification with the aggressor; the former, with its roots in early infancy, is an early mode of perception (Fenichel 1945, p. 37).

14. The part of Mrs. Goforth in *The Milk Train Doesn't Stop Here Anymore* (Williams 1963) was a difficult one for Bankhead, who, at the end of her career, with her own health failing, had to deal with: "Oh, God, Blackie, I'm *scared*. Possibly, maybe, the Boss is — dying this summer! On the *Divina Costiera*, under that, that — angry old lion, the sun" (p. 13). Given the demands of personalizing such a character and what is known of Bankhead's intense relationship to male authority figures (e.g., her grandfather, a United States senator; her father, the 48th speaker of the House; her great admiration for President Kennedy), it is not surprising to come upon such a high degree of ambivalence toward her younger, renowned director.

15. The regression I refer to is a formal one: the actor moves further away from the secondary toward the primary process.

16. This would be an example of countertransference in the director. While I will deal with one aspect of countertransference later on (see chap. 5), my major emphasis is on the actor's transferences onto the director.

17. Of course, looked at in another way, the rage toward the father could make great sense because he suddenly interrupts mother and son in a fight [a sexual encounter]. This is one aspect of the oedipal conflict. Unfortunately, Shakespeare did not write the scene this way. In his wisdom, Shakespeare somehow understood that the absence of rage toward the father suggests the intensity of the castration fears within Hamlet. The rage has to be focused on the mother in order to protect the son from the fearful punishment if he were to acknowledge his tender, loving feelings toward her.

18. The most interchangeable aspect of an instinct is its object (Freud 1915a, p. 122). In an actor's work, the most interchangeable aspect of an objective seems to be its aim.

19. The child is hungry; he cries. Mother does not come; he calls out, "Mommy!" She still does not come. At some point in his development, he may crawl into the kitchen where he finds mother, who fulfills his need. In a rehearsal, Blanche is hungry for Mitch's company; she offers him a drink. He starts to leave. At

some point in the character's development, she gets the idea to abandon the drink, go to Mitch, and remove his jacket; he stays.

In the first instance, at some point prior to the child's autonomous action, his mother may have appeared in the doorway, as it were, showing her child the way. In the second instance, the director performs an analogous function: he chooses the proper moment to intervene in support of the character's needs; he shows her the way.

The director mediates between the character's impulses and the environment of the play so that the character can experience some form of gratification. The director in effect is saying "Mother's in the kitchen" when he whispers to Blanche, "Mitch looks awfully hot and sweaty." Here the director functions as a mother might to help Blanche focus her attention on a meaningful aspect of the environment. However, for the director to say "Take off his jacket" might rob the character of an opportunity to reinforce her ego autonomy just as "Come into the kitchen and you'll get what you want" might to the child. In these latter instances, the "mothering" would err on the side of doing something for the character-child that he could readily do for himself. This would reduce the frustration to such a low level that learning to cope might be inhibited.

20. Sydney Smith (1977) describes "the golden fantasy" as "a regressive reaction to separation anxiety . . . the wish to have all of one's needs met in a relationship hallowed by perfection" (p. 311). He finds such a fantasy reactivated in therapy as the patient begins to face termination.

21. In *Group Psychology and the Analysis of the Ego*, Freud (1921) examined the way in which the leader functioned as an ego ideal. He noted that the mechanism of identification was at work and he differentiated it from an object relationship: the former "to be like," the latter "to have." In a group, identification can coexist with an object relationship as long as the group does not undergo any acute stress. In our terms, the actor can "have his cake and eat it, too," until the group to which he belongs, the cast, undergoes the acute stress of opening night. Then, an object-relationship, in danger of being dissolved, has defensively regressed to an identification of an archaic nature.

22. The psychological mechanisms at work here also have their ancestry in childhood in the structuralization of the superego. At first, the child obeys parental prohibitions out of fear of real punishment. Later, the child internalizes and depersonifies such commands and prohibitions in the form of a newly acquired psychic agency. What was previously an interaction with the

environment has become an intrapsychic conflict; it is the source of the child's conscience, the beginnings of morality. This process of internalization is an outcome of the oedipal conflict in which the child is forced to renounce his incestuous ties to mother and identify with father. The actor-character-child attempts to give up his loving attachment to the opening-phase director (mother) and substitute for it an identification with the useful functions of the final-phase director (father).

This type of resolution of the oedipal conflict is a "positive one." The negative oedipal resolution, where the primary identification takes place with the opposite sex parent, can lead to numerous pathological states. A fuller examination of the psychology of acting would have to take into account the possibility of a negative resolution of the actor-director bond. I suspect that one would see such an outcome in acting students more frequently than in professionals.

23. The change from "get help" to "give him what he wants" suggests a progression from an object relationship typical of the oral phase to one typical of the anal phase. The oral phase can be one of blissful union with mother, while the anal phase ushers in a direct, partly externalized conflict with mother over issues of production and production now. Such issues also dominate the interactions between the actor and director.

As we will see in the following chapters, the actor is also moving through the early developmental stages of anxiety. He must cope with fears about loss of the object and loss of the love of the object. Castration anxiety and moral (superego) anxiety will have to be faced on opening night. The actor's progress along this developmental line is undone as he is about to face the audience when a regression to the earliest forms of anxiety (separation) triggers the traumatic attack of stage fright.

24. Goffman discusses this from a different standpoint. "A completely scripted performance, as found in a staged play, is very effective providing no untoward event breaks the planned sequences of statements and acts; for once this sequence is disrupted, the performers may not be able to find their way back to the cue that will enable them to pick up where the planned sequence had been disrupted. Scripted performers, then, can get themselves into a worse position than is possible for those who perform a less organized show" (1959, p. 228).

25. In Chekhov, for instance, the actor always has the luxury of remaining totally within the imagined circumstances with no need to refer overtly to his audience. In fact, the actor's conviction in the reality of the situation tends to grow on him as the action of the

play proceeds. He can, for example, immerse himself in the palpable reality of the Prozoroff's sitting room. But in Shakespeare, the actor has to oscillate between two modes of performing and these changes in relation to his audience must take place in a split second. Richard III moves from direct address to a private conversation with his brother in the space of one line: "Dive, thoughts, down to my soul—here Clarence comes" (I.i.41). During this one line, the actor has to "reposition" himself from standing on the stage of the theater to a newly created, imaginative place, namely, a street near the Tower of London.

Chapter 3

1. Bergler (1949), a psychoanalyst particularly interested in acting, reports on just such a case.

2. Noel Coward once said that, in order to focus the audience's attention, comedy had to be played in the smallest space possible, in the brightest light and that, on each and every laugh line, the actor must turn directly to the audience before delivering it.

3. Denial is also a primitive mode of defense. Kaplan's first line of symptomatology, in fact, represents more developmentally advanced defense mechanisms; in the later stages of the anxiety attack, the accent shifts from repression to denial, from isolation of affect, intellectualization, reaction formation to projection, introjection, and regression.

4. In metapsychological terms, this selective hypercathexis of appropriately chosen mental representations of self and object within the performing ego diminishes the (attention) cathexis of the mental representation of the audience within the observing ego, promoting the adaptive split, which was referred to at the end of the last chapter.

5. Stage fright may be more intensely felt when an actor is working in a classical play. Here, recourse to poise-enhancing gestures would be near impossible in the sense that our personal mannerisms are contemporary in style and would not fit the universes of *Lear* or *The Misanthrope*. Truly experienced classical actors, however, manage somehow to find stylistically appropriate equivalents. The problem, of course, is always, What do I do with my hands?

Chapter 4

1. According to Fenichel, anxiety can also lead to unpurposeful

innervations and an "inability to achieve normal tonus [because] anxiety paralysis is always spastic" (1928, p. 133).

2. Fenichel noted that "the theater remains the realm of the infantile 'ocular identification'" (1946, p. 356).

3. Artistic representation may also have its roots in psychological mechanisms associated with levels of development preceding the Oedipus conflict. Sharpe (1930) suggests that the artist is "re-creating symbolically the very image that hostility has destroyed" (p. 136). Basing her concept on the investigation of cave paintings and ritual dances of primitive man, she says that "the dead are made alive again by magical acts" (p. 127). The representation of objects in art, then, is an attempt to make reparation for a previously committed, fantasied crime. More specifically, an act of oral destruction (introjective killing by looking at) must be atoned for by a creative act of projection wherein the introject is given life again in the external world in the form of the work of art (see Fenichel 1935). Here, the actor-artist would need the approval of the audience, not to lessen superego anxiety, but to affirm the ascendancy of the libidinal drives over the aggressive ones.

4. The actors' castration anxiety was intensified because its source in their own phallic exhibitionism was reinforced by the "guilty misdeeds" of the characters they had to portray (i.e., the homosexuality).

5. One suspects that this actor was struggling with his incestuous wishes and the guilt that success on stage might entail. This case aptly illustrates the plight of what Freud called "those wrecked by success."

6. See Fenichel 1946, p. 357.

7. Sharpe (1940) discusses the ways in which "metaphor evolves alongside the control of the bodily orifices. Emotions which originally accompanied bodily discharge find substitute channels and materials" (p. 168). Another common phrase for failure is "we just died out there." Schiffer persuasively argues that the creative process involves fantasies of "investing inanimate waste (excrement) with object libido (liveliness) towards the creation of a work of art that symbolizes the resurrection of a lost and mourned object" (1978, p. 148).

8. Along these lines, Fenichel (1946) indicates that "the audience is compelled to give up its spontaneity to accept hypnotically what the actor suggests" (p. 356). In his essay on scoptophilia, he notes that "the 'true' hypnotist . . . lays a spell on his victim by fixing on him an irresistible gaze" (1935, p. 374).

9. As a matter of fact, Bergler (1949) bases his entire theory of stage fright on the notion that exhibitionism is not a partial sexual

instinct at all, but rather, only and always, a defense against voyeurism, i.e., the primal scene. That the actor, to some extent, identifies with the people looking at him, that "through his voyeurism, he peeps at himself" (p. 315), is undoubtedly true, but to go from here to find the sources of stage fright in anxiety related to the actor's primal scene fantasies, as Bergler does, seems to me unwarranted on the basis of the evidence.

Chapter 5

1. Both Fischer (1970) and Rapaport (1960) noted the central importance of separation fears in traumatic, primal anxiety, Fischer directly and Rappaport by implication: is a suitable, need-satisfying object present in the environment? Freud (1926) said that anxiety "has an unmistakable relation to *expectation* [and] a quality of *indefiniteness and lack of object*" (p. 165). And Kaplan distinguishes signal anxiety from primal anxiety, which antici-pates "the violation of the *conditions* guaranteeing life-sustaining supplies" (1969, p. 65).

2. The soliloquy in question begins with the lines "O that this too too solid flesh would melt, / Thaw, and resolve itself into a dew" (I.ii.129), suggesting still another determinant of this actor's anxiety. He is exposed and isolated at the moment when he must refer to (and have made "personal") what amounts to a disintegra-tion of the body-self. The metaphor is extended to include a reference to a merger with mother-earth, expressed in the final phrase, "resolve itself into a dew." Thus, Actor B, like the actors in the prison play, was extremely vulnerable at this point on two counts: both the form and the content of the incident contributed to the upsurge of his anxiety.

3. In his work on elation, Lewin (1950) posited the existence of an oral triad: to eat, to be eaten, to fall asleep. These are a series of fantasies which have their roots in the infant's earliest feeding experiences. "To eat" and "to be eaten" are active in the actor's fantasy life prior to his moment of contact with the audience, while "to fall asleep" speaks to an altered stated of consciousness—a sense in which the actor, in the midst of a successful performance, has moved closer to the primary process, to a dreamlike state. His observing ego, now assured of a fruitful collaboration with the "good" audience can, as it were, relax its vigilance and give full play to the performing self, permitting it greater access to motility and speech.

4. Donald Kaplan goes one step further. He proposes that the

audience participates in the actor's victory over stage fright, a victory which is construed as a creative solution to specific, universal developmental issues. "Stage fright and its vicissitudes can be regarded as a revitalization of a universal developmental plight settled by the audience with residual discontents; the audience now participates in this revitalization as if in a renewed opportunity" (1969, p. 65). And the "universal developmental plight" to which he refers is the separation-individuation process with all its concomitant "residual discontents." This part of Kaplan's discussion is beyond the scope of my present study. To pursue it would demand an analysis of issues related to "the choice of acting as a profession" (Fenichel 1946) as well as an examination of the roots of "performance" in society, i.e., the play as ritual.

REFERENCES

Aristotle. *Poetics*. Trans. J. Hutton. New York: W. W. Norton & Co., 1982.

Bellak, L., M. Hurvich, and H. K. Gediman. 1973. *Ego Functions in Schizophrenics, Neurotics, and Normals*. New York: John Wiley & Sons.

Bennetts, L. 1984. Inside the ensemble of *Hurlyburly*. *New York Times*, 18 July 1984.

Bergler, E. 1949. On acting and stage fright. *Psychiatric Quart. Supplement*, 23(2): 313–19.

Bergman, I. 1978. I confect dreams and anguish. *New York Times*, 22 Jan. 1978.

Blumenthal, E. 1977. Andrei Serban. *Yale/Theatre*, 8(2–3): 66–77.

Bowlby, J. 1973. *Separation*. London: Hogarth Press.

Bradley, B. 1967. *Speech Performance*. Dubuque, Iowa: William C. Brown.

Brenner, C. 1982. *The Mind in Conflict*. New York: International Universities Press.

Brook, P. 1968. *The Empty Space*. New York: Discus Books, 1969.

Burnshaw, S. 1970. *The Seamless Web*. New York: George Braziller.

Burton, R. 1976. I knew if I didn't come back now I never would. *New York Times*, 4 April 1976.

Cottrell, J. 1975. *Laurence Olivier*. Englewood Cliffs, N.J.: Prentice-Hall.

Deutsch, H. 1942. Some forms of emotional disturbances and their relationship to schizophrenia. *Neuroses and Character Types*, pp. 262–81. New York: International Universities Press, 1965.

———. 1955. The imposter; contribution to ego psychology of a type of psychopath. *Neuroses and Character Types*, pp. 319–38. New York: International Universities Press, 1965.

Dorpat, T. L. 1977. Depressive affect. *Psychoanalytic Study of the Child*, 32: 3–27.

Erikson, E. H. 1950. *Childhood and Society*. New York: W. W. Norton & Co.

Fenichel, O. 1928. Organ libidinization accompanying the defenses against drives. *Collected Papers*, first series, pp. 128–46. New York: W. W. Norton & Co., 1953.

――――. 1934. Defense against anxiety, particularly by libidinization. *Collected Papers*, first series, pp. 303–17. New York: W. W. Norton & Co., 1953.

――――. 1935. The scoptophilic instinct and identification. *Collected Papers*, first series, pp. 373–79. New York: W. W. Norton & Co., 1953.

――――. 1945. *The Psychoanalytic Theory of Neurosis*. New York: W. W. Norton & Co.

――――. 1946. On acting. *Collected Papers*, second series, pp. 349–61. New York: W. W. Norton & Co., 1954.

Fischer, W. F. 1970. *Theories of Anxiety*. New York: Harper & Row.

Flugel, J. C.1938. Stage fright and anal eroticism. *British J. of Med. Psychology*, 17: 189–96.

Fonteyn, M. 1976. Her autobiography. *New York Post*, 4 June 1976.

Fowlie, W. 1950. Mystery of the actor. *Yale French Studies*, 3: 5–11.

Freedman, S. G. 1984. Weist and Langella play complex roles in *Fall*. *New York Times*, 5 Nov. 1984.

Freud, A. 1936. *The Ego and the Mechanisms of Defense*. New York: International Universities Press, 1966.

Freud, S. 1900. The interpretation of dreams. *Standard Edition*, 4 and 5. London: Hogarth Press.

――――. 1901. The psychopathology of everyday life. *S.E.*, 6.

――――. 1905*a* (1901). Three essays on the theory of sexuality. *S.E.*, 7.

――――. 1905*b*. Jokes and their relation to the unconscious. *S.E.*, 8.

――――. 1908 (1907). Creative writers and day-dreaming. *S.E.*, 9.

――――. 1910 (1909). Five lectures on psycho-analysis. *S.E.*, 11.

――――. 1910. The antithetical meaning of primal words. *S.E.*, 11.

――――. 1911. Psycho-analytic notes on an autobiographical account of a case of paranoia (dementia paranoides). *S.E.*, 12.

――――. 1914. On narcissism. *S.E.*, 14.

――――. 1915*a*. Instincts and their vicissitudes. *S.E.*, 14.

――――. 1915*b*. The unconscious. *S.E.*, 14.

――――. 1920. Beyond the pleasure principle. *S.E.*, 18.

————. 1921. Group psychology and the analysis of the ego. *S.E.*, 18.

————. 1922. Some neurotic mechanisms in jealousy, paranoia and homosexuality. *S.E.*, 18.

————. 1926. Inhibitions, symptom and anxiety. *S.E.*, 20.

Funke, L., and J. E. Booth. 1963. *Actors Talk about Acting*, vol. 1. New York: Avon Books.

Funke, P. 1982. Stage fright. *Playbill*, April.

Gabbard, G. 1979. Stage fright. *Int. J. Psychoanal.*, 60: 383–92.

————. 1983. Further contributions to the understanding of stage fright: Narcissistic issues. *J. Amer. Psychoanal. Assn.*, 31: 423–41.

Gelb, B. 1977. Great Scott! *New York Times Magazine*, 23 Jan.

Gilder, R. 1926. La nostalgilder: Some letters of Eleonora Duse. In R. Gilder et al., eds., *Theatre Arts Anthology*, pp. 252–60. New York: Theatre Arts Books, 1950.

Goffman, E. 1959. *The Presentation of Self in Everyday Life*. Garden City, N.Y.: Doubleday Anchor Books.

Greenacre, P. 1958*a*. The imposter. *Emotional Growth*, 1: 93–112. New York: International Universities Press, 1971.

————. 1958*b*. The relation of the imposter to the artist. *Emotional Growth*, 2: 533–54. New York: International Universities Press, 1971.

Greenson, R. R. 1967. *The Technique and Practice of Psychoanalysis*, vol. 1. New York: International Universities Press, 1968.

Grotowski, J. 1968. *Towards a Poor Theatre*. New York: Simon & Schuster.

Guntrip, H. 1969. *Schizoid Phenomena, Object-Relations and the Self*. New York: International Universities Press, 1970.

Hall, P. 1984. *Peter Hall's Diaries*. Ed. J. Goodwin. New York: Harper & Row.

Harbage, A. 1955. *Theatre for Shakespeare*. Toronto: University of Toronto Press.

Hartmann, H., E. Kris, and R. M. Lowenstein. 1946. Comments on the formation of the psychic structure. *Psychoanalytic Study of the Child*, 2: 11–38.

Hoffer, W. 1949. Mouth, hand and ego-integration. *Psychoanalytic Study of the Child*, 3–4: 49–56.

Jacobson, E. 1964. *The Self and the Object World*. London: Hogarth Press, 1965.

Kaplan, D. 1968. The primal cavity. *Drama Review*, T39: 105–16.

————. 1969. On stage fright. *Drama Review*. T45: 60–83.

Kaplan, L. J. 1978. *Oneness and Separateness: From Infant to Individual*. New York: Simon & Schuster.

Kernberg, O. 1975. *Borderline Conditions and Pathological Narcissism*. New York: Jason Aronson.

Kohut, H. 1971. *The Analysis of the Self*. New York: International Universities Press.

Kris, E. 1952. *Psychoanalytic Explorations in Art*. New York: International Universities Press.

Leavy, S. A. 1970. John Keats' psychology of creative imagination. In E. Kurzweil and W. Phillips, eds., *Literature and Psychoanalysis*, pp. 201–16. New York: Columbia University Press, 1983.

Levinson, P., et al. 1978. Causes for the premature interruption of psychotherapy by private practice patients. *Am. J. Psychiatry*, 135(7): 826–30.

Lewin, B. D. 1950. *The Psychoanalysis of Elation*. New York: Psychoanalytic Quarterly, 1961.

Little, S. W., and A. Cantor. 1970. *The Playmakers*. New York: W. W. Norton & Co.

Loewald, H. W. 1978. Primary process, secondary process, and language. In J. H. Smith, ed., *Psychoanalysis and Language*, pp. 235–70. *Psychiatry and the Humanities*, vol. 3. New Haven and London: Yale University Press.

Mahler, M. S., F. Pine, and A. Bergmann. 1975. *The Psychological Birth of the Human Infant*. New York: Basic Books.

Menninger, K. 1958. *Theory of Psychoanalytic Technique*. New York: Science Editions, 1961.

Meredith, B. 1970. In Little and Cantor 1970.

Mitgang, H. 1983. When actors review the audience. *New York Times*, 21 April 1983.

Modell, A. H. 1976. "The holding environment" and the therapeutic action of psychoanalysis. *J. Amer. Psychoanal. Assoc.*, 24: 285–307.

Moore, B. E., and B. D. Fine. 1968. *A Glossary of Psychoanalytic Terms and Concepts*, 2d ed. New York: American Psychoanalytic Association, 1978.

Moramarco, S. S. 1976. Stage fright . . . and how to beat it. *Toastmaster*, 42(12): 5–7.

Olivier, L. 1982. *Confessions of an Actor*. New York: Penguin Books, 1984.

Osborne, J. 1957. *The Entertainer*. New York: Criterion Books, 1958.

Probst, L. 1975. *Off Camera*. New York: Stein & Day, 1978.

Rangell, L. 1954. The psychology of poise, with special elaboration on the psychic significance of the snout or perioral region. *Internat. J. of Psychoanal.*, 35: 313–32.

Rapaport, D. 1960. *The Structure of Psychoanalytic Theory*. Psychological Issues, Monogr. 6. New York: International Universities Press, 1969.

Ross, L. and H. Ross. 1962. *The Player: A Profile of an Art*. New York: Simon & Schuster.

Saint-Denis, M. 1960. *Theatre: The Rediscovery of Style*. New York: Theatre Arts Books.

———. 1982. *Training for the Theatre: Premises and Promises*. Ed. by S. Saint-Denis. New York: Theatre Arts Books; London: Heinemann Educational Books.

Sandler, J., and B. Rosenblatt. 1962. The concept of the representational world. *Psychoanalytic Study of the Child*, 17: 128–45.

Schiffer, I. 1978. *The Trauma of Time*. New York: International Universities Press.

Seldes, M. 1978. *The Bright Lights: A Theatre Life*. Boston: Houghton Mifflin.

Sharpe, E. F. 1930. Certain aspects of sublimation and delusion. *Collected Papers on Psychoanalysis*, pp. 125–36. London: Hogarth Press, 1968.

———. 1940. Psycho-physical problems revealed in language: An examination of metaphor. *Collected Papers on Psychoanalysis*, pp. 155–69. London: Hogarth Press, 1968.

Sheldon, E. K. 1967. *Thomas Sheridan of Smock-Alley*. Princeton: Princeton University Press.

Siebers, T. 1983. *The Mirror of Medusa*. Berkeley, Los Angeles, London: University of California Press.

Skinner, B. F. 1972. On "having a poem." *Saturday Review of Literature*, 15 July 1972, pp. 32–35.

Skinner, O. 1938. Kindling the divine spark. In R. Gilder et al., eds., *Theatre Arts Anthology*, pp. 277–84. New York: Theatre Arts Books, 1950.

Smith, S. 1977. The golden fantasy: A regressive reaction to separation anxiety. *Internat. J. of Psychoanal.*, 58: 311–24.

Stanislavski, C. 1936. *An Actor Prepares*. New York: Theatre Arts Books, 1952.

Stapleton, M. 1960. Interview. In L. Funke and J. E. Booth, eds., *Actors Talk about Acting*, 2: 86–120. New York: Avon Books, 1963.

Thomas, A. 1982. The fear of being "on stage": Interview by S. H. Anderson. *New York Times*, 25 Jan. 1982.

Thorndike, S. 1932. I look at the audience. In R. Gilder et al., eds., *Theatre Arts Anthology*, pp. 300–303. New York: Theatre Arts Books, 1950.

Van Druten, J. 1945. The job of directing. In R. Gilder et al., eds.,

Theatre Arts Anthology, pp. 535–40. New York: Theatre Arts Books, 1950.

Waelder, R. 1967. Inhibitions, symptoms and anxiety: Forty years later. *Psychoanalysis: Observation, Theory, Application*, pp. 338–60. New York: International Universities Press, 1976.

Weissman, P. 1969. Creative fantasies and beyond the reality principle. *Psychoanal. Quart.*, 38: 110–23.

Wilder, B., C. Brackett, and D. M. Marsham, Jr. 1950. "Sunset Boulevard." Hollywood: Paramount Pictures, unpublished screenplay.

Wiles, T. J. 1980. *The Theater Event: Modern Theories of Performance*. Chicago and London: University of Chicago Press.

Williams, T. 1947. *A Streetcar Named Desire*. New York: New Directions.

———. 1955. Cat on a hot tin roof. *The Theatre of Tennessee Williams*, 3: 1–215. New York: New Directions, 1971.

———. 1963. The milk train doesn't stop here anymore. *The Theatre of Tennessee Williams*, 5: 1–120. New York: New Directions.

———. 1975. *Cat on a Hot Tin Roof*. New York: New Directions.

Winnicott, D. W. 1951. Transitional objects and transitional phenomena. *Collected Papers*, pp. 229–42. London: Tavistock Publications, 1958.

———. 1952. Anxiety associated with insecurity. *Collected Papers*, pp. 97–100. London: Tavistock Publications, 1958.

———. 1960a. Ego distortion in terms of true and false self. *The Maturational Processes and the Facilitating Environment*, pp. 140–52. New York: International Universities Press, 1966.

———. 1960b. The theory of the parent-infant relationship. *The Maturational Processes and the Facilitating Environment*, pp. 37–55. New York: International Universities Press, 1966.

Wittels, F. 1939. Unconscious phantoms in neurotics. *Psychoanal. Quart.*, 8: 141–63.

INDEX

Abandonment, fear of, 86

Accidents: in rehearsal, 37; on stage, 63, 67. *See also* Blooper lore; Mistakes in rehearsal

Acting: vs. acting out, 43–44; anal-sadistic component of, 94–96; British vs. American, xiv–xv; and emotion, 5; as reacting, 57

"Acting sense," 31

Actor, 10, 24, 39–40, 52, 75, 87, 108; defenses of, against regression, 44–45; dependency needs of, 19–20, 32–33; as instrument, 1–9; performing, 53–58; rehearsing, 21–38, 55; self-evaluation by, 1; student, 5

Actors' Fund benefit shows, 121

Actors Studio, 113

Actor-audience relationship, erotic imagery for, 68

Actor-manager, 12, 18

Adaptive regression, 76

Ad lib, 63

Affective memory, 10–11. *See also* Emotion memory

After the Fall, 48–49

Aggression, actor's, 73–75, 90–91, 97–101

Alcohol, 60, 99, 100

Alexander technique, 125

Allen, Rae, 98, 123

American Academy of Dramatic Arts, 18

Ambitendency, 111

Ambivalence toward director, actor's, 40

Ancestry vs. identity, 85

Antoine, André, 18

Anxiety, x, 22, 44, 80; castration, 85, 91, 134, 138, 140; vs. depression, 102; disintegration, 117; paralysis in, 139; preparation as defense against, 75–77; primal vs. signal, 141; and ritual, 72–74; separation, 84–85, 106–8, 114, 138; signal, 80–81, 141; symptoms of, 83

Archie Rice (*The Entertainer*), 101

Aristotle, 9, 88

Art as reparation, 140

Ashcroft, Peggy, 6, 128

Asides, 58

Atkinson, Brooks, 69

Audience, 57, 100; actors' fantasies about, 70, 109–10; actors' wish to control, 68–69; of fellow actors, 121–22; as holding environment, 117; indifferent, 120, 126; as medium for reintegration, 118; "thoughtless hunger" of, 96–101

Author. *See* Playwright